THE
SOUTHWE
BED &
BREAKFAST
GUIDE

El Paradero, Santa Fe, New Mexico

ARIZONA, NEW MEXICO, TEXAS

Bed & Breakfast Guide

SOUTH   WEST

BY LUCY POSHEK

Photographed by Lucy Poshek

DESIGNED AND PRODUCED BY
ROBERT R. REID AND TERRY BERGER

PRENTICE HALL TRAVEL

NEW YORK   LONDON   TORONTO   SYDNEY   TOKYO   SINGAPORE

Front cover photograph: *Mi Casa Su Casa, Scottsdale, Arizona*
Frontispiece photograph: *Adobe staircase at Casa Europa, Taos, New Mexico*

The photographs in this book
have been supplied by the
bed and breakfasts selected
for the book.

Published by Prentice Hall General Reference
A division of Simon & Schuster, Inc.
15 Columbus Circle
New York, NY 10023-7780

PRENTICE HALL and colophon are registered trademarks of Simon
& Schuster, Inc.

A Robert Reid Associates production
Typeset in Bodoni Book by Monotype Composition Company, Baltimore
Produced by Mandarin Offset, Hong Kong
Printed in Hong Kong

1 2 3 4 5 6 7 8 9 10

Library of Congress Cataloging-in-Publication Data
Poshek, Lucy.
    Bed & breakfast guide. Southwest : Arizona, New Mexico,
Texas / by Lucy Poshek ; photographed by Lucy Poshek.
       p.   cm.
    Includes index.
    ISBN 0-671-84952-2
    1. Bed and breakfast accommodations—Southwest, New—
Guidebooks.
  2. Southwest, New—Guidebooks. I. Title. II. Title: Bed
and breakfast guide, Southwest.
TX907.3.S69P67   1992   92-24998
647.947903—dc20   CIP

CONTENTS

ARIZONA

NEW MEXICO

TEXAS

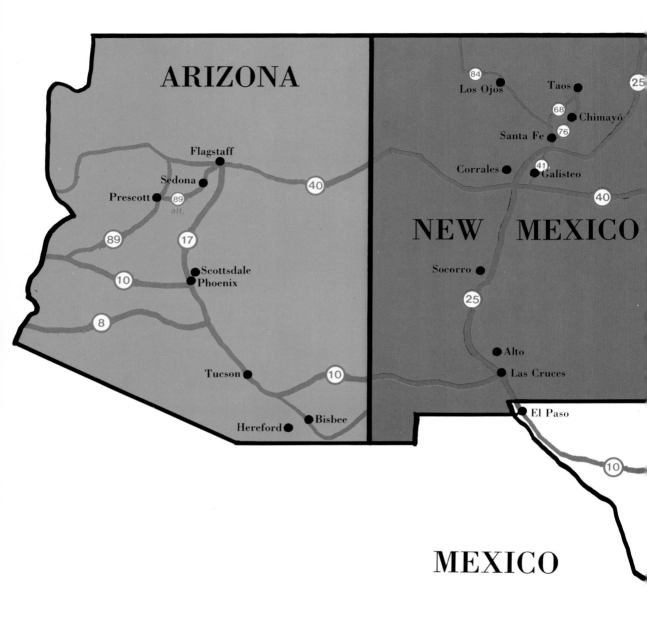

ARIZONA

Flagstaff

Sedona

Prescott ● 89 alt.

89

17

10

8

Scottsdale
Phoenix

Tucson ●

10

Hereford ● ● Bisbee

NEW MEXICO

84 Los Ojos ● Taos ● 25

68 ● Chimayó

Santa Fe ● 76

Corrales ● ● 41 ● Galisteo

40

Socorro ●

25

● Alto
● Las Cruces

● El Paso

10

MEXICO

NOTE: all the bed and breakfasts
described in this book are to be
found in the cities and towns
shown on this map.

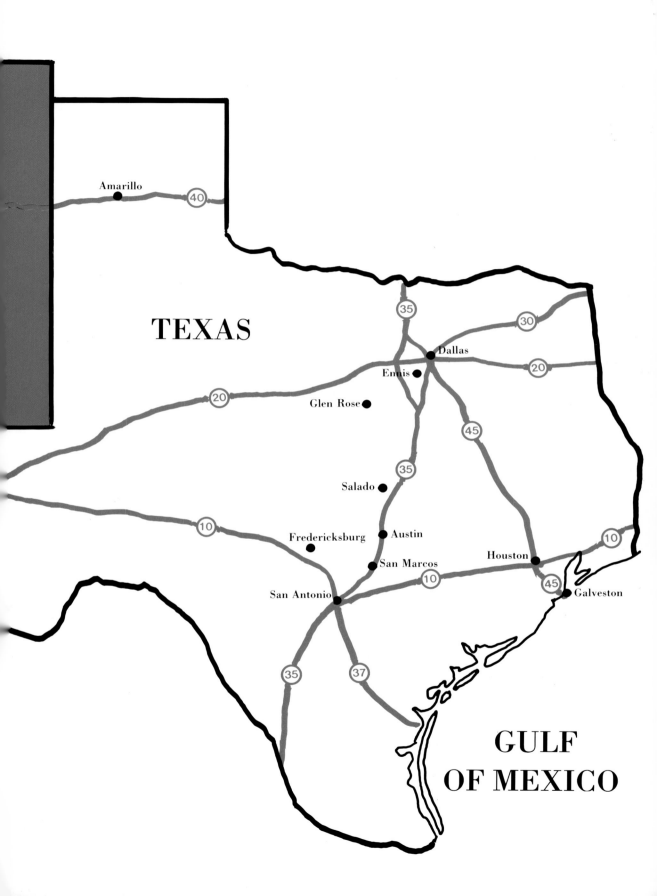

RED ROCKS OF SEDONA

Arizona

RAMSEY CANYON INN

Hummingbird heaven

Some mornings the bird watchers are lined up outside Ramsey Canyon Inn at dawn with their binoculars aimed high. Now and then an excited cry rises in the crisp morning air as a "birder" spots a painted redstart, ruby-crowned kinglet, yellow-bellied sapsucker, or one of the fourteen species of hummingbirds indigenous to the area.

Set alongside a shady canyon stream in the heart of Southeastern Arizona—known as the foremost birding spot in the U.S.—Ramsey Canyon Inn is just a few steps from the Nature Conservancy's Mile Hi/Ramsey Canyon Preserve. Over two hundred species of birds and wildlife have been sighted within the preserve.

When guests tire of walking and birding they can return to the inn and help themselves to a slice of innkeeper Shirlene DeSantis' prize-winning pie. She bakes pies fresh daily with apples, peaches, and cherries from her own orchard.

Guests gather around an early morning breakfast table (where hummingbirds fly right to the feeder at the window) for a heartwarming meal of Dutch or German apple pancakes, quiche or fritatas, sausages, muffins, sliced fresh fruit, juice, and coffee.

The two-story main house has seven neat-as-a-pin bedrooms furnished with antiques, pretty floral quilts, dried flower arrangements, and wall stenciling done by Shirlene. Also in the main house is a comfortable living room with a fireplace and informative books about "hummers." On Ramsey Creek there are two modern housekeeping cottages, each with a fully-equipped kitchen, bathroom, living room, and bedroom.

From April to October, Shirlene has been known to go through four gallons of sugar water daily in her fourteen feeders. And just when birding season winds down, the maple, sycamore, and oak-filled canyon turns brilliant with fall foliage.

Left, owners Shirlene and Ron DeSantis with their dog Megan.

RAMSEY CANYON INN, 31 Ramsey Canyon Road, Hereford, AZ 85651; (602) 378-3010; Shirlene DeSantis, owner. Open all year. Seven rooms and 2 housekeeping cabins, all with private baths. Rates: $75 to $85, including full breakfast and afternoon pie. Children over 12 accepted; no pets; smoking restricted to patio. No credit cards. Mesquite Tree recommended for dining. Birding, hiking, and rockhounding nearby.

DIRECTIONS: From Sierra Vista, take Hwy. 92 about 6-1/2 miles south to Ramsey Canyon Rd. and turn right. Inn is about 3-1/2 miles up Ramsey Canyon Rd.

A place for serious bird watchers.

The carved oak bed in Room 5.

BISBEE GRAND HOTEL

Where Intrigue and Mystery abound

The year is 1927. You are Constance Desmond, a former entertainer at a speakeasy called the Pitty Pat Club. Your boyfriend is Ramon Navaro, who may be having an affair with another woman. You arrive at the Bisbee Grand Hotel in your flapper dress for a weekend rendezvous with other members of the Southwestern Sleuth Society who share equally shady roles. And, as fate will have it at a murder mystery, someone bites the dust. Only after a weekend of inquests, comical games, and some wicked tangos is the murderer at last revealed.

It's all part of the intrigue at the Bisbee Grand Hotel, where spirited owners Gail Waid and Bill Thomas direct "Murder Mystery" weekends throughout the year. The mysteries range among six different time periods, from 1886 to 1968. Guests remain in character all weekend and take part in one zany event after another, including a "Lack-of-Talent Talent Show."

The hotel, with its adjacent Western saloon, ladies

Left, above. *The hotel fronts on Bisbee's Main Street. Below, "Murder Mystery" guests adopt a 1920s theme.*

Guest rooms open off the second floor foyer.

The grandly elegant Victorian Suite.

parlor, and melodrama theatre, is a perfect setting for such goings-on. Once a turn-of-the-century boarding house for miners, the hotel has a classic Old West Victorian look—plush red carpeting, red velvet, elaborately patterned wallpaper, and brass beds. Gail has added many of her own family heirlooms, such as handmade quilts and lace handkerchiefs, to their collection of antiques.

Each of the ten guest rooms features a slightly different period theme, from a Hunter's Room complete with riding crop and hunting cap, to an Oriental Suite outfitted with luxurious Chinese furnishings. The Victorian Suite, with its claw-footed tub and elegant sitting room, is another favorite.

In the morning, guests awaken to the smell of Gail's spicy blend of coffee, which she serves along with a full breakfast out on the balcony overlooking Bisbee's old-fashioned Main Street.

BISBEE GRAND HOTEL, A BED & BREAKFAST INN, 61 Main Street, Box 825, Bisbee, AZ 85603; (800) 421-1909; (602) 432-5900; Gail Waid and Bill Thomas, owners. Open all year. Eight rooms and 3 suites: 3 rooms have sinks and share 2 baths; the remaining rooms have private baths. Rates: $50 to $95, including full breakfast. Smoking allowed outside and in saloon only; adult-oriented; no pets. Visa/MasterCard/American Express. Saloon and theatre on premises. Wine Gallery, Stenzel's, and 18 Steps recommended for dining. Copper mine tour, historic city tour, shops, and art galleries nearby. Six miles from Mexican border.
DIRECTIONS: From Hwy. 80 south, take Old Bisbee exit. Hotel is on Main St. in downtown Bisbee.

The Queen Room.

PARK PLACE B&B

Decidedly informal and homey

Park Place Bed & Breakfast, a 1919 Mediterranean style home, is located in a quiet, tree-lined residential area just ten minutes from the historic mining town of Bisbee. Its five-thousand-square-feet accommodate four spacious guest rooms and a terrace upstairs, plus a downstairs living room, dining room, library, garden patio, and sun porch.

Hosts Bob and Janet Watkins stay busy around the year catering weddings and organizing weaving workshops at their inn. Park Place is one of several B&B's in Bisbee that sponsor three and five-day fiber seminars such as tapestry making, spinning, and cloth

Left, a charming breakfast setting of German pancakes with apples and whipped cream.

Samples of Janet Watkin's weaving and loom, located on the sun porch.

designing. Bob and Janet keep several large harness looms in their pleasant sun porch, where the light is at its natural best.

Park Place is decidedly informal and homey. Janet, who ran an antique store for several years, says, "Antiques are nice, but they just aren't comfortable." She has opted for contemporary furnishings in three of the guest rooms, one of which features a waterbed. Her fourth bedroom is the only exception—in pink, white and mauve, it contains an eclectic array of antiques and a claw-footed tub.

Bob and Janet, both Bisbee natives, ran a restaurant in town together for more than seven years and still love gourmet cooking. As a special treat for guests on their first day, Bob whips up delicious, puffy German pancakes topped with home-canned apples, whipped cream, and mint. The second morning they enjoy a Southwestern scrambled egg enchilada made with locally grown chiles; their third day blue corn Belgian waffles.

Once fueled by a three-course breakfast, guests can drive into old Bisbee for an underground tour of the Copper Queen Mine or a day of exploring antiques shops and craft galleries. Nestled a mile high in the Mule Mountains with a near-perfect climate, Bisbee has become a popular refuge for artists and retirees.

PARK PLACE BED AND BREAKFAST, 200 East Vista, Bisbee, AZ 85603; (800) 388-4388; (602) 432-3054; Bob and Janet Watkins, owners. Open all year. Four rooms, 2 with private baths and 2 sharing a bath. Rates: $35 to $55, single; $40 to $60, double, including full breakfast. Children not encouraged; pets not encouraged; smoking allowed outside. Visa/MasterCard. Biking, horseback riding, cactus botanical gardens, art galleries, golf, tennis, and Mexico nearby.

DIRECTIONS: From Hwy. 80 south, at Bisbee traffic circle, take Bisbee Rd. (sign says to Hospital). Turn left on Congdon, then right on E. Vista. Inn is on the corner of E. Vista and Tener.

An upstairs guest room decorated with antique christening dresses.

THE JUDGE ROSS HOUSE

Collections galore

The Judge Ross House is a sweet surprise in an unassuming neighborhood outside of old Bisbee. The two-story red brick home, built in 1908 by a superior court judge, is delightfully decorated with country Victorian antiques and lovely collectibles.

Hosts Jim and Bonnie Douglass are a loving, active couple who have opened their home to guests since 1985. Bonnie, an Arizona native, also owns an antiques shop in Bisbee and is an on-call bank teller, while Jim ("who has only lived in Arizona for thirty-seven years, so he's not a native yet," jokes Bonnie), has two other jobs as well.

Upstairs, two cheerful bedrooms—one in pink and one in blue—share a family room (filled with books, TV, and VCR), a sun porch, and large bathroom with plenty of complimentary toiletries. The blue room is

Left, above. *Owner Bonnie Douglass holding her dog Annie.* Below. *View of upstairs guest room and bathroom.*

especially pretty, with starched, white christening dresses—one from a Paris flea market and another that belonged to the most famous "madam" in El Paso— ornamenting the walls. A large third bedroom is available downstairs on a two-night basis only.

Throughout the house are Bonnie and Jim's collections—antique milk bottles from Southwestern dairies, teddy bears, baby shoes, delicate beaded purses, a 1920s wood stove, and paintings by local artists.

Bonnie's breakfast specialties include three-cheese stuffed French toast with ginger peaches, Belgian waffles or eggs Benedict, along with fresh fruit, muffins, ham, sausage, coffee, and juice. Depending upon the season and guest preferences, she may serve breakfast on the upstairs sun porch, in the dining room, or out on the patio, which sometimes serves as the setting for small receptions and weddings.

THE JUDGE ROSS HOUSE, 605 Shattuck Street, Bisbee, AZ 85603; (602) 432-4120; Jim and Bonnie Douglass, owners. Open all year. Three rooms: 1 with private bath, 2 sharing a bath. Rates: $55, single; $60 to $65, double, including full breakfast. No children; no pets; no smoking. Visa/MasterCard. Wine Gallery recommended for dining. Hiking, bird watching, mineral and rock collecting, antiques shops, and copper mine tour nearby.

DIRECTIONS: From Hwy. 80 south, at Bisbee traffic circle, take Bisbee Rd. (sign says to Hospital). Turn left on Cole Ave. and then right where it dead-ends at Shattuck. Inn is first house on right.

Room Four, at breakfast time.

THE GREENWAY HOUSE

A painstakingly restored mansion

As a former Rough Rider with Teddy Roosevelt and manager of the Calumet & Arizona Mining Company, John C. Greenway and his wife, Isabella (who later served two terms in Congress), were prominent citizens of Bisbee. In 1906, they built a twenty-eight room mansion in the quiet neighborhood of Warren, across Bisbee's rough-and-tumble Brewery Gulch.

The Craftsman-style mansion and its carriage house contain eight guest rooms and suites, all with private baths and kitchenettes stocked with welcome refreshments and provisions for a continental breakfast (homebaked blueberry muffins are also delivered to the door in the morning). Nice extras such as fluffy white robes, hair dryers, fruit baskets, and chocolate candies are found in every room.

The guest quarters in the main house are filled with antiques and patchwork quilts. Room Three features a high walnut headboard, while another room sports a

Left, below. *Room Three, with its Victorian furnishings and magnificent walnut bed.*

sleigh bed. Room Four has a fresh, cheerful appearance, with white wicker furniture, white brass bed, and a blue, pink and white Wedding Ring quilt. The carriage house, which houses two family-sized suites, is furnished more informally.

Downstairs is a game room for the guests, complete with billiard table, TV, and 1940s Wurlitzer. Ask innkeeper Joy O'Clock to take you on a tour of the rest of the grand mansion, which she painstakingly restored with co-owner Dr. George Knox. (Removing ten thousand square feet of carpeting to expose the wood floors was only one of the monumental renovation tasks they tackled.) Their private quarters—including an impressive foyer, living room and dining room of dark woodwork, pressed copper ceilings, Tiffany lamps, and original stenciling—are available for small group meetings, weddings, and dinners.

THE GREENWAY HOUSE, 401 Cole Avenue, Bisbee, AZ 85603; (800) 253-3325; (602) 432-7170; Dr. George S. Knox and Joy O'Clock, owners. Open all year. Eight rooms and suites, all with private baths and kitchenettes; 2 suites are in separate Carriage House. Rates: $75 to $125, including continental breakfast and welcome refreshments; extra person $15. Children permitted in Carriage House; no pets; no smoking; Spanish spoken. Visa/MasterCard. Golf (9-holes), tennis, hiking, bird watching, and mountains nearby.

DIRECTIONS: From Hwy. 80 south, at Bisbee traffic circle, take Bisbee Rd. (sign says to Hospital). Turn left at Copper Queen Hospital, which is Cole Ave. Up hill, inn is third large house on left.

VIEW POINT B&B

"Välkommen"

View Point is an unpretentious, affordable bed and breakfast in the quiet northern part of Tucson. The two-level home has a sweeping view from the Catalina foothills down to the city—twenty minutes away—and the impressive desert mountains are temptingly close.

Owners Bill and Clara Vancura live in their own private quarters on the upper level, while guests have a separate entrance downstairs, by a solar-heated swimming pool. Sliding glass doors open from the patio to a guest living room and breakfast area, where there is a stone fireplace, comfortable couch and rockers, along with a TV, VCR, kitchenette, books, and bowls of pretzels. The four guest rooms emanating from this common area are tastefully furnished (with top-of-the-line mattresses) and free of clutter.

Little Swedish touches (Clara's family is Scandinavian) are scattered throughout View Point, from the "Välkommen" welcome sign outside, to Clara's inspired breakfast specialty—Swedish pancakes with imported lingonberries and sour cream. Her breakfasts range from continental to full, depending on guest prefer-

Left. The pool, with Santa Catalina Mountains.

Swedish pancakes with lingonberries and sour cream.

ences. Some of her dishes include heart-shaped waffles topped with fruit, hearty casseroles, juicy grapefruit straight off the tree, and homemade Swedish rye bread.

Sabino Canyon, only fifteen minutes away in the Coronado National Forest, is a big draw for locals and visitors alike.

VIEW POINT BED AND BREAKFAST, Represented by Mi Casa Su Casa, P.O. Box 950, Tempe, AZ 85280-0950; (800) 456-0682; (602) 990-0682; Bill and Clara Vancura, owners. Open all year. Four rooms: 2 with private baths; 2 with shared bath. Rates: $50 to $60, single; $55 to $65, double, including full breakfast. Children over 8 accepted (swimmers only); no pets; smoking allowed outdoors only. No credit cards. El Corral, Anthony's, Keaton's, and Club 21 recommended for dining. Swimming pool on premises. Sabino Canyon nearby.

DIRECTIONS: Located in north Tucson. Directions given upon confirmation.

Detail, showing Marjorie's silver hairbrush set.

PEPPERTREES B&B INN

English hospitality in the Southwest

This red-brick Victorian home derives its name from two large old peppertrees which dominate the front yard. Their fragrance, plus the surrounding rosemary, jasmine, and orange blossoms envelop the house in a welcoming perfume.

Innkeeper Marjorie Martin, originally from the Cotswolds, combines English hospitality with a taste of the Southwest at Peppertrees. While her home is furnished with family heirlooms from England, two separate guesthouses called Sunrise and Sunset feature a Southwestern motif. Afternoon tea is highlighted by scrumptious old-fashioned shortbread, while at breakfast guests might feast on blue corn pancakes or Mexican cornbread with turkey sausage.

Both two-story guesthouses offer spacious quarters—each with two bedrooms, full kitchens, living rooms, washers and dryers—off a flowered-filled courtyard

Left, above. *Owner Marjorie Martin and her B&B.* Below. *The Veranda room.*

with a stone fountain. The Veranda Room, in the main house, has a lovely, more delicate feel. Light streams through an abundance of windows onto a white wrought-iron bed, romantic floral spread, bedside table covered with Battenburg lace and fragrant flowers.

With three professional chefs in Marjorie's family, food is underscored at Peppertrees. As she says, "If you send people away with a full and happy tummy, they're going to remember you." Out of response to guest requests for her recipes, Marjorie wrote her own cookbook which has already sold out its first printing. Her recipes reflect the style of Peppertrees—Southwest flavors (such as chorizo balls and tortilla pancakes) with an English accent. The inn's thriving orange and lemon trees provide fresh ingredients for Marjorie's homemade jams and syrups—another Peppertrees specialty.

PEPPERTREES B&B INN, 724 East University Boulevard, Tucson, AZ 85719; (800) 348-5763; (602) 622-7167; Marjorie G. Martin, owner. Open all year. Rates: $78 to $140 in winter; $68 to $110 in summer; $10 less for single occupancy; includes full breakfast and afternoon tea. Five rooms, 1 with private bath: 1 room in main house; 4 rooms in 2 separate guesthouses. Children accepted in guesthouses only; smoking allowed on patio only; no pets; French and Spanish spoken. Visa/MasterCard. Delectables, Café Sweetwater, Caruso's, and Café Tierra Cotta recommended for dining. University of Arizona and Arizona State Museum nearby.

DIRECTIONS: From I-10, exit at Speedway and drive east toward University of Arizona. Turn right on Stone Ave., then left on University Blvd. Inn is 7 blocks down University Blvd. on right.

At the breakfast table.

EL PRESIDIO B&B INN

A jewel

Patti and Jerry Toci spent more than a decade meticulously restoring their 1886 American Territorial home—a unique Victorian adobe in the heart of Tucson's historic El Presidio district. Searching remote villages of Mexico for the right craftsmen and historically authentic materials was, as Patti says, "a task almost too difficult to hurdle." But a walk through this now completed, award-winning jewel leaves no question that their painstaking efforts were handsomely rewarded.

At the center of El Presidio is a traditional Southwestern *zaguán*—an airy, high-ceilinged hall—which Patti has turned into a stunning antiques-filled living room. Off the *zaguán* is The Victorian Suite, with its cheerful parlor, fireplace, white wicker furnishings, and French doors leading out to the garden. In separate tile-roofed buildings off the courtyard are the converted Gate House and Carriage House Suites, both impeccable and beautifully decorated.

Equally impressive are El Presidio's grounds, carved

Left, above. *Looking across the courtyard to the Carriage House.* Below. *El Zaguán (living room).*

stone fountains, and cobblestoned courtyard. Filled with magnolias, pines, mesquite and fruit trees, lush floral displays, Victorian herbs, and chile *ristras*, this tranquil courtyard is where guests inevitably congregate.

Patti demonstrates a genuine love for her guests that makes even a brief stay a memorable experience in hospitality.

No where is this more evident than at her superb gourmet breakfasts which she presents on fine china and linens in the Veranda Room overlooking the courtyard. Guests are pampered with such sublime pleasures as French toast stuffed with bananas and almond butter, or sweet potato Belgian waffles topped by sautéed apples and yogurt, always accompanied by fresh fruit, bacon, coffee, juice, and a variety of divinely moist muffins.

EL PRESIDIO BED & BREAKFAST INN, 297 North Main Avenue, Tucson, AZ 85701; (602) 623-6151; Patti Toci, owner. Open all year. Rates: $60 to $80, single; $75 to $100, including full breakfast and evening refreshments. Four rooms and suites, including a separate carriage house suite; all rooms have private baths; 2 suites have kitchenettes. One child over 12 accepted in Carriage House Suite only; no pets; smoking allowed outside only. No credit cards. Bicycles and guest membership at health club provided. In El Presidio Historic District near arts district and downtown Tucson; museums, restaurants within walking distance.

DIRECTIONS: From I-10, exit at St. Mary's Rd. and drive east. Turn right on Main Ave. Inn is on corner of Main and Franklin.

Zelda's Room.

LA POSADA DEL VALLE

Southwest art deco

Having opened in 1986, La Posada del Valle set the standard as the first among an ever-growing number of outstanding B&B's in Tucson. From its flowered courtyard to its lovely art deco interior, the inn is, as one guest wrote, "a delightful oasis in the middle of Tucson."

La Posada del Valle, meaning "Inn of the Valley," is a 1929 one-story southwestern home designed by Josias T. Joesler, a renowned Tucson architect. The all-white exterior, large windows, and pastel furnishings give the inn a light, airy feel. Its surrounding courtyard is landscaped with palms, fragrant orange trees, bougainvillea, and colorful spring bulbs.

Owner Debbi Bryant cheerfully greets guests with afternoon tea and homebaked goodies in a long, graceful living room enhanced by understated tones of mauve, grey and salmon, floor-to-ceiling bookshelves, and several striking bronzes (one, the "Winged Victory," signed by Charles Sykes, is the hood ornament for the Rolls-Royce.) Guests are also drawn to the inn's nostalgic 1932 radio.

In keeping with the art deco theme, all five bedrooms are named after a famous woman from the 20s and 30s: Zelda Fitzgerald, Sophie Tucker, Claudette Colbert, Isadora Duncan, and Pola Negri. Some of the bathrooms feature art deco tilework. Sophie's Room boasts an 1818 king-sized bed that once belonged to a fan dancer at Tombstone's Crystal Palace.

Left. *The inn is built around a courtyard.*

Weekday guests (many of whom are visiting the nearby university and medical center) have a continental-plus breakfast—homebaked goods, cereal, fruit, juice, coffee and tea—in the dining room or wicker-filled sun room. On weekends, Debbi and her husband Charles whip up more elaborate dishes, such as cream cheese blintzes with raspberry sauce, or vegetable strudel with parmesan cheese sauce, along with bacon and sausage. Every evening, beds are turned down and a chocolate placed on the pillow.

LA POSADA DEL VALLE BED & BREAKFAST INN, 1640 North Campbell Avenue, Tucson, AZ 85719; (602) 795-3840; Debbi Bryant, owner. Open all year. Five rooms, all with private baths. Rates: $90 to $115, including full breakfast on weekends and continental plus breakfast on weekdays; summer discounts available. Children over 12 preferred; no pets; no smoking; Spanish spoken. Visa/MasterCard. Guest privileges at Tucson Racquet Club included. Arizona-Sonora Desert Museum, Old Tucson Movie Location, and Old Mexico recommended for sightseeing.

DIRECTIONS: From I-10, exit at Grant Rd. Drive east and turn right on Campbell Ave. Turn left on Elm St. and then immediately right into inn's parking lot.

The sitting room.

Maria's great-great grandparents' rosewood bed and the Governor's Room.

The bathtub, with a mysterious pair of shapely legs.

BRIMSTONE BUTTERFLY

A Special serenity

There is a special serenity to Maria Johnstone's 1930s adobe home in Tucson. Soothing classical music and cream-colored sofas await guests in the refreshingly cool living room. Through the tall windows is an inviting pool framed by brilliant bougainvillea.

Maria's tasteful collection of rustic Pennsylvania Dutch furnishings are in perfect harmony with this Southwestern home. And everything—from the extra-long church pew-turned-coffee table, to her hand-designed needlepoint pillows, to the foyer's whimsical, butterfly-ornamented tree—has been created and placed with an imaginative eye.

If the house isn't enough to slow you down, Maria (pronounced MarAYEa) herself will take care of that. A licensed massage therapist, she will perform massages with advance notice. That, plus a dip in her extra-deep, plant-enveloped bathtub usually renders guests unable to do much more than lift a finger.

Left, above. *The pool, deck, and patio area is the focal point of the inn.* Below. *The living room and Oliver, the dog.*

Two rooms—The Cabaña and The Studio—are in separate guest houses with private entrances. The Governor's Room, in the main house, has an adobe fireplace and four-poster, rosewood bed that once belonged to Maria's great-great grandfather (who was the first ambassador to Brazil and later the governor of Ohio). A set of steps leads up to the high bed, which is romantically sheathed in white—sheer white curtains, white eyelet spread, linens, and pillows.

In each of the rooms is a welcome packet of information and complimentary chocolate butterfly. Among the brochures is a breakfast menu from which guests can make selections. The attractively-presented breakfast includes fresh-squeezed orange juice, a generous slice of seasonal fruit, coffee, hot-out-of-the-oven popovers, and either a choice of cereals or eggs Florentine.

THE BRIMSTONE BUTTERFLY, 940 North Olsen Avenue, Tucson, AZ 85719; (602) 322-9157; Maria P. Johnstone, owner. Closed July. Three rooms, including a separate cabana, all with private baths; one room has fireplace. A fourth bath has extra-large tub. Rates: $82, single; $98, double, including full breakfast and afternoon refreshments. Children are responsibility of parents; pets considered; smoking not allowed in bedrooms; Swiss German, German, French, Czechoslovakian, and Spanish spoken. No credit cards. Complimentary use of Tucson Racquet Club included and, at extra charge, massages at the inn. Swimming pool on premises. University of Arizona nearby.

DIRECTIONS: From I-10, exit at Speedway Blvd. Drive east past University of Arizona to Olsen Ave. (2 blocks past Campbell Ave.) and turn right. Inn is 2 blocks south of Speedway Blvd.

Owners Val and Mae Robbins

RIMROCK WEST

East meets West

For over twenty years Mae and Val Robbins owned a resort in Pennsylvania called Rimrock East. Then, on a visit to Arizona, they fell in love with the "starkly beautiful expanse of the Southwest." So, they packed away the Poconos for twenty acres in the foothills of northeast Tucson. And, the name of their bed and breakfast hacienda? What else, but Rimrock West!

Rimrock West is a place of real seclusion; an ideal spot to come and paint the dramatic desert scenery and flint-colored mountains. Footpaths meander among the palo verdes, mesquite, and saguaros, where sounds of exotic desert birds are interrupted only by the call of a coyote.

The low-lying, 1960s adobe hacienda with its whimsical, turquoise-painted grillwork is built around a Spanish-style courtyard and trickling fountain. Two bedrooms are on the courtyard, or guests can opt for more privacy in a separate adobe house down by the pool.

Every room is filled with a lifetime of artwork—bronzes, paintings and enamels created by Val, Mae and son Christopher—most of which is for sale.

Breakfast in the courtyard features southwestern eggs with salsa, or corn soufflés, or pancakes, along with vegetable muffins and whipped fresh fruit juice. During the winter, fragrant pecan logs burn twenty-four hours a day in the living room fireplace.

RIMROCK WEST, 3450 North Drake Place, Tucson, AZ 85749; (602) 749-8774; Mae D. Robbins, owner. Open September 1 to June 1. Three rooms and suite, all with private baths: 2 rooms in main house and 1 adobe guest house. Rates: $85 to $115, including full breakfast; extra person $20. No children; one small dog allowed; no smoking; some Spanish spoken. No credit cards. Jerome's, Olive Tree, and Solarium recommended for dining. Swimming pool, hiking, and bird watching on premises. Sabino Canyon, Mt. Lemmon, horseback riding, and golf nearby.

DIRECTIONS: From Tucson Airport, turn right on Valencia Rd. Turn left on Alvernon Way, which becomes Golf Links Rd. Turn left on Wilmot Rd., which turns into Tanque Verde Rd. Turn left on Catalina Hwy., drive one mile, then turn right on Prince Rd. After another mile, turn right on N. Drake Pl. Hacienda is at the end of N. Drake Pl.

A pool is de rigueur *in the Southwest.*

CASA ALEGRE B&B INN

Honoring Tucson's history

The living room

Casa Alegre, which means "Happy House," is a new Tucson B&B, having opened in 1992. Although located on a very busy street near the University of Arizona, the sturdy Craftsman-style bungalow is virtually sound-proof.

Owner Phyllis Florek, a former bank manager, is very excited about her switch to innkeeping. She has given the 1915 home a facelift with new landscaping and fresh white paint, punctuating the deep eaves with blue and pink trim. The living and dining areas are handsomely appointed with a stone fireplace, lots of built-ins, antiques, and Oriental carpets.

Phyllis has highlighted a different part of Tucson's history in each of her four guest rooms. Rose Quartz features mining memorabilia—an old carbide lantern, hard hat and hand-hewn shovel—that once belonged to Phyllis's father when he was a miner. The Spanish Room has an unusual queen-sized headboard that was handmade in Mexico for a priest. The Amethyst Room, with its claw footed tub, has a Victorian theme, while the Southwestern-style Saguaro Room has a rustic lodgepole bed.

Afternoon refreshments and munchies are served out by a small swimming pool. For breakfast, Phyllis cooks up hearty, creative breakfasts varying from oat bran pancakes and apples fried with bacon, to upside-down French toast, to bread pudding and raisin bread topped by strawberries and ham.

Tucson's clean, dry air, manageable size, and great number of cultural and natural attractions are a delightful surprise to many first-time visitors. Among its top landmarks are the Arizona-Sonora Desert Museum (an outstanding natural zoo), the Mission San Xavier del Bac (the "White Dove of the Desert"), Saguaro National Monument, the Museum of Art, and Kitt Peak National Observatory.

CASA ALEGRE BED & BREAKFAST INN, 316 East Speedway Boulevard, Tucson, AZ 85705; (602) 628-1800; Phyllis Florek, owner. Open all year. Four rooms, all with private baths. Rates: $65 to $75, single; $70 to $80, double, including full breakfast and afternoon refreshments. Children considered on case-by-case basis; smoking allowed outside only. Visa/MasterCard. Swimming pool on premises. Golf, tennis, museums, and art galleries nearby.

DIRECTIONS: From I-10, exit at Speedway Blvd. and drive one mile east. Inn is on the southeast corner of Speedway Blvd. and 5th Ave.

Left, above. *The exterior, showing the owner, Phyllis Florek.* Below. *The exotic bed and the Spanish Room.*

The refreshing pool.

Left, *The back yard pool, patio, and house.*

The beautiful Thunderbird Room.

WESTWAYS RESORT INN

Very luxurious; muchas amenities

The "Private" in Westways Resort is in earnest. When the Spanish Mediterranean home first opened in 1987, it served as a secluded retreat for high-powered corporate executives. Owner Darrell Trapp did everything possible to preserve their sense of privacy, and his Phoenix home still draws many business people and celebrities who are looking for a low-profile, comfortable getaway.

The interior is contemporary with Southwestern accents. A large sunken living room and Arizona room (recreational den) share a fireplace and high vaulted ceilings. Six spacious bedrooms emanate from these common areas. Through the sliding glass doors are a pool, hot tub, fitness room and patio with lounge chairs and complementary towels.

Breakfast, which guests select from a menu, features a different entrée each day, such as Belgian pecan malted waffles or "mucho grande" omelets. Generous munchies—homemade chile, tamales, chicken wings, or ice-cream sundaes—are set out in the afternoon.

Situated in a modern residential area of far-northern Phoenix, Westways appears at first to be rather isolated from the rest of the city. But within a ten-minute drive are two million-dollar sports clubs (one at which Westways guests have membership privileges), three golf courses, and a surprising number of fine restau-

rants. Westways also provides mountain bikes for trips to the hilly desert preserve of nearby Thunderbird Park.

If guests opt to stay in for dinner, they can request a "rent-a-chef"—a chef from the Arizona Biltmore, no less—to come over and whip up an intimate gourmet dinner. Taking indulgence one step further, massages can also be arranged at incredibly reasonable prices.

WESTWAYS "PRIVATE" BOUTIQUE RESORT B&B INN, P.O. Box 41624, Phoenix, AZ 85080; (602) 582-3868; Darrell Trapp, innkeeper. Open all year. Six rooms, all with private baths. Rates: $49 to $122, including full breakfast (deluxe continental in summer) and afternoon refreshments. Reservations required at least 24 hours in advance. Catered dinner and massages available at extra charge. Children discouraged; no pets; smoking allowed in restricted areas; Spanish, German, and some French spoken. Visa/MasterCard/American Express. Swimming pool and hot tub on premises. Mountain bikes and country club privileges provided. Surrounded by a desert mountain preserve.

DIRECTIONS: Located in northwest Phoenix in an executive estate area. Directions given upon confirmation.

The living room.

Breakfast in a basket.

MARICOPA MANOR

Join the extended family

Mary Ellen and Paul Kelley obviously enjoy having lots of people at the Manor. After raising twelve children, they further extended their family by opening their home to bed and breakfast guests. In every room is a welcome book which begins: "When at the Manor, you are a part of our family."

Their 1928 Spanish-style home has an impressive approach, with its curved driveway and graceful archways. To the side is a tranquil courtyard and fountain surrounded by palms, orange trees, and trailing flowers. In the back, on the immense lawn, are bird houses, a gazebo spa, and a wonderfully gnarled, sixty-year-old palo verde—the state tree of Arizona.

The formal foyer, embellished with delicate alabaster statues, is flanked by an eighteenth-century French-style living room and music room which contains unusual antique instruments. As one wanders through the house back to the more casual gathering room, the décor becomes decidedly more relaxed.

Two of the suites are in the main house and three are in separate guest houses on the grounds. Each suite features a different theme, from the ultra-modern Reflections Future to the traditional Victorian Suite. The Library Suite—a favorite of guests—has a comfortable den with desk, TV, phone, and shelves of beautiful leatherbound classics.

Maricopa Manor is located close to downtown Phoenix and a mind-boggling number of restaurants, making it a popular draw for business people. With their business guests in mind, Mary Ellen and Paul developed a unique "breakfast in a basket" that is brought to the door in the morning. The picnic basket, which contains linens and all the ingredients for an elegant breakfast, allows guests the freedom either to eat in total privacy or mingle with others outdoors.

MARICOPA MANOR, 15 West Pasadena Avenue, Phoenix, AZ 85013; (602) 274-6302; Mary Ellen and Paul Kelley, owners. Open all year. Five suites, all with private baths: 2 suites in main house; 3 suites in separate guest houses. Rates: $59 to $99, including continental plus breakfast. Children welcome; no pets; smoking allowed in designated areas only. No credit cards. A multitude of restaurants nearby, many within walking distance. Hot tub on premises. Golf, tennis, fitness center, and downtown Phoenix nearby.

DIRECTIONS: From I-17, exit at Camelback Rd. and drive east. Turn left on 3rd Ave., then right on Pasadena Ave.

Left, below. *The bedroom to the Library Suite.*

A bedroom in the guest house.   *The exterior is shown on the front cover.*

MI CASA SU CASA

A fabulous modern adobe

There is a softness to the Sonoran desert that is nowhere more enhanced than at this fabulous contemporary adobe. Designed by renowned Scottsdale artist William Tull, the seven-thousand-square-foot home is like a sculpted work of art. Walls undulate, rooms flow into one another, and every line is softly curved.

Owner Ramón Vives, a restaurateur originally from Spain, spared no expense on this stunning home which he helped build ten years ago. (Making over two hundred-thousand adobe bricks was one of the no-minor-tasks involved.) Elisa Green, his companion and interior decorator, has blended together a bold ensemble of massive furnishings and striking artwork—paintings, pottery, baskets—from Mexico, Spain and the Southwest. In the living room brightly-colored, overstuffed Guatemalan pillows and throws mingle with sheepskin rugs on black leather couches, while masked Hopi Indians look down from their colorful canvases.

Left, above. The pool, showing the house on the right and the guest house on the left. Below. The living room.

The décor in every meandering room and alcove is truly exciting.

Palm trees on an immaculate lawn surround the pool. Next to it is a separate, southwestern-style guest house. The pool pavilion features a hi-tech stereo system, large-screen TV, steam sauna, and showers. Another of many artfully concealed TV's is built right into the adobe wall of a tiled, outdoor Jacuzzi. There is also an exercise room, an oversized private tennis court, and no less than nine adobe fireplaces, or *chimeneas*, throughout.

All of the homes in this exclusive Pinnacle Peaks area of northern Scottsdale enjoy ample breathing space. Beyond the electronic gates and low adobe walls is an expanse of quiet, natural desert landscape punctuated by huge cacti and the peaceful sounds of birds and wildlife.

This home must be seen to be believed. It is an extraordinary, luxurious, private retreat.

REPRESENTED BY MI CASA SU CASA, P.O. Box 950, Tempe, AZ 95280-0950; (800) 456-0682; (602) 990-0682; Ramón Vives, owner. Open all year. Four rooms, including separate one-bedroom guest house with kitchen; all rooms with private baths. Rates: $100 to $150, including continental plus breakfast. No children; no pets; smoking permitted outside only; 6 languages spoken. No credit cards. Swimming pool, jacuzzi, steam room, and private tennis court on premises.

DIRECTIONS: In Pinnacle Peak area of Scottsdale. Directions given upon confirmation.

The Garden Room.

PLEASANT STREET INN

A cool escape from desert heat

Hard to believe, but when this 1913 Prescott home was threatened with demolition not so long ago, all two hundred thousand pounds of it were moved just one block in order to save it. By the time Jean Urban bought the two-story house in 1991, it had been totally restored and remodeled, full of bed and breakfast potential.

The interior of Pleasant Street Inn, neat as a pin, is designed in a fairly traditional English motif, with tones of blue, mauve, and rose throughout. Handsome Ethan Allen furnishings are set before the fireplace in the all-blue front parlor/living room. The two spotless bedrooms and two suites feature English floral spreads.

Of breakfast, Jean says she works very hard to provide her guests with personalized service and cater to any special dietary needs. In the dining room, at the game table, or out on the pleasant front terrace, she serves a fresh fruit dish, homebaked goods such as poppy seed bread or "glorious morning muffins"—made with apples, carrots, raisins and nuts—and a main dish (stuffed French toast, perhaps). Her special cream-cheese honey butter makes a tantalizing, frequent appearance on the table.

Prescott's mile-high elevation is a cool relief to many Arizonans who come here to escape the desert heat. They often wind up out on the porch of the Pleasant Street Inn for afternoon beverages and hors d'oeuvres. From there, the three-block walk to Courthouse Square passes through Prescott's most historic section, with its turn-of-the-century homes and antiques shops.

PLEASANT STREET INN, 142 South Pleasant Street, Prescott, AZ 86303; (602) 445-4774; Jean B. Urban, owner. Open all year. Four rooms, including two suites, all with private baths. Rates: $70 to $120 in winter; $80 to $120 in summer. Includes full breakfast. Children accepted; no pets; no smoking. Visa/ MasterCard. Hassayampa Hotel, Murphy's, and Gurley St. Grill recommended for dining. Hiking, fishing, golf, and biking nearby.

DIRECTIONS: Three blocks south of Gurley St. (Hwy. 89) and two blocks east of Prescott's Courthouse Square.

VICTORIAN INN

Elegant breakfasts

During the 1890s, Victorian homes were hard to come by in a remote territory such as Arizona. They usually arrived piece-by-piece on trains from the East. So, innkeeper Tamia Thunstedt is rightfully proud of the authentic details of her Victorian Inn of Prescott: the seventeen original chandeliers, sliding wood doors and woodwork, stained-glass windows and original hardware, to name a few.

During Christmas (Prescott is Arizona's "Christmas City"), over ten thousand lights are strung across the two-story inn, taking about sixty man-hours to accomplish. All this, plus its resplendent blue and white exterior, fish scale shingles and turret makes the Victorian Inn a real town showcase.

The cream-flowered wallpaper and mauve carpets are punctuated throughout the inn by cranberry-rose accents, from the antique velvet chairs in the front parlor to the chiffon bed canopy and satin sheets in Eve's Garden Room. The large Victoriana Suite, with its fine carved bed and fireplace mantel, is the most

Left, below. *The Victoriana Suite.*

The animals provide night-time company.

Staircase landing with stained-glass window.

popular of the four upstairs guest rooms.

Lace nightgowns and handmade dolls are for sale in the foyer. In keeping with the Victorian theme, Tamia's mother made old-fashioned dresses which they sometimes wear at the inn.

An elegant sit-down affair, breakfast is presented in a cozy dining room on antique china, linens, and gold-plated utensils. Blueberry-buttermilk Swedish pancakes, Canadian bacon, stratas, orange custard French toast (It soaks overnight—"It just melts in your mouth," says Tamia), and raspberry Linzer muffins are Victorian Inn specialties. In summer, there's also fresh fruit and yogurt; in the winter, a warm fruit compote such as apples and amaretto.

The Victorian Inn is less than a block from Prescott's historic Courthouse Square.

VICTORIAN INN OF PRESCOTT, 246 South Cortez Street, Prescott, AZ 86303; (602) 778-2642; Tamia S. Thunstedt, owner. Open all year. Four rooms, including one suite. Suite has private bath; rooms share hall bath. Rates: $90 to $125, including full breakfast. Children discouraged; no pets, no smoking. Visa/MasterCard. Murphy's and Hassayampa Hotel recommended for dining. Historic buildings, antique shops, and museums nearby.

DIRECTIONS: One block south of Prescott's Courthouse Square on the corner of Cortez and Carlton Sts.

A cottage interior.

BRIAR PATCH INN

A wooded paradise

Nature abounds at the Briar Patch Inn, a collection of fifteen lovely cottages nestled deep in Sedona's Oak Creek Canyon. Oak Creek surges right by the cottages, while squirrels, deer, sheep, and even peacocks gambol over nine acres of wooded grounds.

Guests are immediately drawn to the creekside log benches and chairs, where one could spend hours basking in the quiet, soothing environment. Gravel pathways meander among the sycamores, oaks and lilacs, with an inviting wooden swing here and there.

All of the cottages, decorated in tastefully rustic Arizona Indian and Mexican furnishings, feature a different lay-out. Some are on the creek while others are set back on the grass. Most have kitchens and, best of all, cozy fireplaces that are stocked with wood, ready to go.

Owners JoAnn and Ike Olsen have taken this wooded paradise one step further by adding a cultural dimension: Classical concerts by the creek (every other Friday evening and every morning during breakfast) and music appreciation workshops are offered to guests during the summer months.

Breakfast—a healthy affair of whole wheat breads, granola, juice, fruit, yogurt, hard or soft-boiled eggs, and coffee—can be taken out by the creek or enjoyed in a cozy fireside lounge, with its library of books about the Southwest. Afternoon refreshments include winter hot cider, summer iced tea, and always fresh-baked cookies.

The Briar Patch is not only peacefully romantic, but great for families, too. Children can swim in a ten-foot-deep swimming hole nearby, hike, or visit with Willie and Nillie, two of the inn's friendly black sheep. The peacock is mostly penned up nowadays, ever since he had an embarrassing encounter with a black Porsche—spotting his reflection in its shiny surface, he thought it was another bird and drew his beak right down the door!

BRIAR PATCH INN, Star Route 3, Box 1002, Sedona, AZ 86336; (602) 282-2342; JoAnn and Ike Olson, owners. Open all year. Fifteen cottages, all with private baths and fireplaces. Rates: $98 to $165, including full breakfast and afternoon refreshments; extra person $25. Children accepted; no pets; smoking limited; Spanish and German spoken. Visa/MasterCard. Hiking, fishing, swimming in Oak Creek, birdwatching, and creative arts workshops on premises.

DIRECTIONS: Three miles north of Sedona on the right off Hwy. 89A in Oak Creek Canyon.

Left. *The magnificent peacock showing off near the office.*

Oak Creek is nature at its most stunning.

A guest room suite.

SADDLE ROCK RANCH

A favorite movie set

Poised on a hillside above West Sedona, Saddle Rock Ranch takes full advantage of its breathtaking red rock vistas. The panoramic view forms a mesmerizing, almost fantasy backdrop to the poolside patio. The same scene can be glimpsed from the large living room picture windows.

Constructed of native materials—red rock and adobe walls, flagstone floors and beamed ceilings—the house once served as the main lodge for a 6,000-acre dude ranch. Featured in such Old West films as "Broken Arrow" and "The Texas Trail," it was also a favorite movie site of the 1940s and '50s.

Now slimmed down to three acres, Saddle Rock is a bed-and-breakfast inn with an emphasis on romance. Innkeepers Fran and Dan Bruno, both former managers at the Ritz Carlton, welcome their guests with hand-written notes, afternoon cheese and heart-shaped

Left, above. *The pool is set amid majestic scenery. Below. The living room, with dogs Fergie and Diana.*

crackers, breakfasts of blue-corn heart-shaped waffles, and evening turn-down service. The rock fireplaces in all three suites are lit in the winter, while a Jacuzzi, cascading into the pool, draws guests in the summer. Before touring Sedona for the day, guests leave with oatmeal cookies that Fran and Dan have baked.

On display in the airy living room are collections of local art and Hopi Indian pottery, an 1850s pump organ and "Nipper," their RCA Victor dog. Dan also has one of the foremost collections of police badges in the world, numbering over a thousand by now.

The Saddle Rock Suite boasts another commanding view, while the Rose Garden Room looks onto a flowery terraced hillside. Up the hill is the Cottage, formerly a cowboy bunkhouse and artist's studio.

Having only three suites in such a prime tourist spot, Saddle Rock Ranch often books up several months ahead during the high season, so advance reservations are recommended.

BED & BREAKFAST AT SADDLE ROCK RANCH, P.O. Box 10095, Sedona, AZ 86336; (602) 282-7640; Fran and Dan Bruno, owners. Open all year. Three rooms with fireplaces and private baths. Rates: $90 to $115, single; $95 to $125, double, including full breakfast and afternoon refreshments. Children over 13 accepted; no pets; smoking allowed outdoors only; Spanish, French, Italian and German spoken. No credit cards. Rene's and Pietros recommended for dining. Swimming pool on premises. Hopi Mesa and jeep tours, hiking, horseback riding, and tennis nearby.

DIRECTIONS: Map and directions given upon confirmation.

Owners Bob and Lynne Gillman, with Fudge and Kate.

COZY CACTUS B&B

Stunning views of Sedona's red rocks

"Our goal is to make people feel at home and comfortable," says innkeeper Bob Gillman. That's why he and his wife, Lynne, selected the name Cozy Cactus for their bed and breakfast in Sedona.

Their two dogs, Kate and Fudge, greet guests at the door of the modern, ranch-style home, setting an informal tone right away. Entering the living and dining areas, guests are taken aback by breathtaking views of Sedona's red rock formations.

In fact, the patio of Cozy Cactus opens right out to the Coconino National Forest, providing miles of uninterrupted wilderness hiking through the mesquite and manzanita. Castle Rock is just a stone's throw away, as are Bell Rock and Courthouse Butte. Nearby Wild Horse Mesa, the setting for many old John Wayne movies, is another well-known landmark.

Each pair of bedrooms shares a sitting room with fireplace and kitchen. The two sitting rooms also face the patio, where refreshments are served in the afternoon. Guests can spot local wildlife—quail, roadrunners and hummingbirds—while watching the rocks change to a rich red with the setting sun.

Left. *A real Southwest setting.*

Early risers who wish to go for a hike and "commune with nature" can fuel themselves with before-breakfast coffee. Bob and Lynne's health-conscious breakfasts begin with a fresh fruit cup such as baked bananas or baked pears stuffed with walnuts and raisins. Next, it's turkey sausages or turkey "ham" and such entrées as whole wheat buttermilk raspberry pancakes (no sugar), baked French toast supreme, or "feather bed" eggs made with pears and cream cheese.

Lynne and Bob are a warm, friendly couple who both have professional theater backgrounds—they met in an Indiana repertory playhouse. Since they are now active in Sedona's community theaters, it's no surprise to see many of their guests at the local plays.

COZY CACTUS BED & BREAKFAST, 80 Canyon Circle Drive, Sedona, AZ 86336-8673; (800) 788-2082; (602) 284-0082; Lynne and Bob Gillman, owners. Open all year. Four rooms, all with private baths. Rates: $85, single; $90, double, including full breakfast and afternoon refreshments. School-age children accepted; no pets; smoking restricted to patios; Italian and American sign language spoken. Visa/MasterCard. Heartline Cafe, Shugrue's, and Mandarin House recommended for dining. Direct access to Coconino National Forest. Hiking, birdwatching, golf, tennis, and community theatres nearby.

DIRECTIONS: From I-17, take Hwy. 179-Sedona exit. Drive 6.4 miles toward Sedona and turn left on Bellrock Blvd., then right on Canyon Circle Dr. Inn is on right.

The dining room.

The American Room.

The magnificent villa complex.

CANYON VILLA B&B INN

State-of-the-art

Canyon Villa could serve as an archetypal model for anyone building a bed and breakfast from scratch. This brand new state-of-the-art inn in Sedona is a long-awaited realization for Chuck and Marion Yadon, who spent years researching the perfect location, attending seminars, and visiting other establishments to learn the "inns" and outs of innkeeping. A tour of their inn will show that all of their homework paid off.

Down to the last detail, Canyon Villa has been designed with maximum comfort and privacy in mind. Every one of the ten rooms has arched French doors opening to a private patio or balcony with unrestricted views of Sedona's famous red rocks. The private baths

Left, above. *The spacious, luxurious sitting room. Below. Owners Chuck and Marion Yadon.*

feature whirlpool-tubs and terry robes. TVs and phones are hidden away in armoires. Bedrooms are extra-soundproofed (even the plumbing is sound-insulated) and can be individually, quietly cooled or heated. One room offers full handicapped facilities.

Early-riser coffee is offered to guests, as well as a full breakfast of Marion's special cinnamon rolls and breads, fruit, and varied entrées such as sour cream waffles, pumpkin pancakes, or an egg and meat dish. Afternoon appetizers are served by the pool. Turn-down service includes bedtime treats.

Through the tall arched windows of the spacious dining and living rooms and from the swimming pool just outside are more fabulous panoramas. In addition to a large fireplace the two common rooms share, there is another fireplace out by the pool.

Bedroom décor runs the gamut from Victorian to Southwestern to Oriental. "Spanish Bayonet," with its romantic tub and fireplace, is a good honeymooner choice. "Ocotillo" is the most rustic-looking room, whereas the distinctly Victorian "Evening Primrose" features Marion's antique family bed.

CANYON VILLA BED & BREAKFAST INN, 125 Canyon Circle Drive, Sedona, AZ 86336; (800) 453-1166; (602) 284-1226; Chuck and Marion Yadon, owners. Open all year. Ten rooms, all with private baths; some rooms with fireplaces and whirlpool tubs. One room offers full handicapped facilities. Rates: $95 to $135; $10 less for single occupancy; $25 for extra person; includes full breakfast and afternoon appetizers. Children not encouraged; no pets; no smoking. Visa/MasterCard. L'Auberge and Fournos recommended for dining. Direct access to Coconino National Forest. Swimming pool on premises. Guests have membership privileges at Sedona Racquet Club. Hiking, golf (2 championship courses), hot air ballooning, art galleries, shopping nearby.

DIRECTIONS: From I-17, take Hwy. 179-Sedona exit. Drive 6.4 miles toward Sedona and turn left on Bell Rock Blvd., then right on Canyon Circle Dr.

The comfortably cool living room.

THE INN AT FOUR TEN

Light and airy at 7000 feet

Flagstaff's proximity to the natural wonders of the Grand Canyon, Sedona, and Oak Creek Canyon make it a convenient base for Northern Arizona sightseeing. But most visitors never wade past the freeway motels to Flagstaff's appealing historic downtown. There, one can find everything from a delightful vegetarian restaurant, to a cozy corner bookstore, to an immaculately restored bed and breakfast called the Inn at Four Ten.

The crisp grey and white trimmed inn was built in 1907 by a wealthy Wisconsin banker-rancher. After surviving a number of owners, including a university fraternity house, the structure was transformed into a bed and breakfast inn by Carol and Mike Householder in 1991.

Country quilts, dried flower wreaths, and antiques are displayed throughout the house. The cheerful guest rooms and suites, some with private outside entrances, are named after important women in Carol's life.

Left, below. *Kathleen's Suite.*

Kathleen's Suite, a favorite with guests, has Southwestern furnishings, a kiva fireplace, sitting room, and kitchen. Rabbits are grouped in Karolyn's Suite, while other bedrooms feature Shaker, twig, or nautical motifs.

The wraparound porch, patio, and gazebo make an attractive setting for small receptions, weddings, and summer breakfasts. During cooler months, breakfast is served in a sunny room where the tables have been cleverly constructed out of old-fashioned sewing machine bases. Blue and white striped sofas, lace curtains, and Oriental carpets on light wood floors give the adjoining living room an inviting effect, too.

The Amtrack station is only four blocks from The Inn at Four Ten. A half-dozen downtown restaurants are within walking distance. Nights are crisp here, and the snow-covered San Francisco peaks behind Flagstaff are a scenic reminder of the city's seven-thousand-foot elevation.

THE INN AT FOUR TEN, 410 North Leroux Street, Flagstaff, AZ 86001; (602) 774-0088; Carol and Mike Householder, owners. Open all year. Nine rooms, including 6 suites with private baths and 3 rooms, 2 of which share a bath. Rates: $45 to $69 in winter; $55 to $79 in summer; $5 less for single occupancy. Includes full breakfast and afternoon refreshments. Children accepted; no pets; smoking allowed outside only. No credit cards. Near University of Northern Arizona and historic downtown. Skiing, fishing, and horseback riding nearby.

DIRECTIONS: From I-40 take 195B exit north to Flagstaff, go under train tracks and take 3rd left at Leroux Street for 4½ blocks.

MUSEUM OF FINE ARTS, SANTA FE

New Mexico

The R.C. Gorman Room, with its kiva fireplace.

LUNDEEN INN OF THE ARTS

A Mexican Territorial inn

Jerry and Linda Lundeen have managed to blend their bed and breakfast, art gallery, and devotion to Southwestern culture so thoroughly together that it's impossible to separate the three. Every wall of this historic Las Cruces adobe is lined with paintings, most of which are for sale. Each guest room is named after a famous New Mexican or Indian artist and decorated accordingly.

While Linda runs the gallery, Jerry, an architect and lay minister (he performs weddings at the inn), often conducts week-long group seminars about Southwest architecture and literature, weaving, coiled pottery, silversmithing, and hands-on adobe-making. Outside, he has built a *horno*, or Indian oven, where bread is baked and sometimes served to guests in the afternoon.

This creatively-designed Mexican Territorial inn actually consists of two, two-story buildings that are connected by a vast living room. Dark hardwood floors, eighteen-foot pressed-tin ceilings, an 1855 German piano, and some Jacobean-style furnishings lend a pleasing Old World ambience to the living room, while the tall arched windows and large painting (most notably, those by Ken Barrick) are distinctly contemporary.

With seventeen widely different bedrooms (Jerry is building more casitas out back, as well), Lundeen's is good for groups as well as individual guests. Among the most memorable rooms are Maria Martinez, with its vigas-and-latillas Anasazi headboard (which Jerry constructed himself) and Georgia O'Keefe, in black, white, and grey, with calla lilies on the mantel. R.C. Gorman, which has its own entrance, features a kiva fireplace and partial viga ceiling.

Both New Mexico natives (Jerry grew up on an Indian reservation), Jerry and Linda share a special knowledge and deep love of Southwestern culture that inspires their guests and keeps them coming back.

Left. *Gallery/dining area, with its minstrels' gallery, fine antiques (including a German piano), and a variety of paintings.*

The Maria Martinez Room.

LUNDEEN INN OF THE ARTS, 618 South Alameda Boulevard, Las Cruces, NM 88005; FAX (505) 526-3355; (505) 526-3327; Linda & Jerry Lundeen, owners. Open all year. Seventeen rooms and casitas, all with private baths; some rooms with fireplaces and kitchenettes. Rates: $53 to $58, single; $57 to $105, double, including full breakfast and afternoon refreshments. Long term accommodations available. Children limited; pets considered if owners provide kennel; smoking limited; Spanish spoken. Visa/MasterCard/American Express. Art gallery and lecture room on premises. Las Cruces cultural historic district and La Mesilla nearby; farmers market 2 days a week.

DIRECTIONS: From I-10, exit at La Mesilla and turn left on Avenida de Mesilla, going east toward the mountains. Turn left on Main St., then left on Alameda where the street divides. Inn is 2 blocks north on left.

SIERRA MESA LODGE

A mountain resort

The wooded mountains around Ruidoso, in south-central New Mexico, are a real surprise to most first-time visitors. A departure from the state's usual desert mesas, this idyllic mountain resort has it all—skiing in winter, horseracing in summer, and brilliantly colored aspens in the fall.

Just a short drive out of Ruidoso, nestled on a few acres of hillside, is the Sierra Mesa Lodge. Owners Larry and Lila Goodman designed, built and decorated this bed and breakfast inside and out. From the wood trim to the porcelain fixtures, their inn shows meticulous attention to detail.

The five pretty guest rooms, most with window seats facing the woods or forested mesa, are equally elegant, appointed in romantic country themes: Victorian, French Country, Oriental, Queen Anne, and Country Western. The soundproofed bedrooms all have down comforters and pillows. In some rooms there are dolls handmade by Lila. Extra touches include flowers, chocolates, ice buckets, toiletries for "forgetful guests," and kimonos for trips to the indoor hot tub. From there, guests can bubble away in total privacy with windows open to the pines.

Coffee and cake are offered in the afternoon, as are evening wine and cheese by the living room fire. Guests benefit from Lila and Larry's love of gourmet cooking (they have even written their own cookbook) during their generous breakfasts, which can be enjoyed in the dining room or in bed. Heated grapefruit, strawberries Romanoff, or yogurt parfaits start the day, followed by a main dish such as croissant French toast or blintze soufflés.

Guests can work off their blintzes by hiking up into the forest for a mountain panorama or golfing. Some prefer just settling into a rocker on the front porch with Magnum, the dog, or Ethel and Buff, the resident cats.

The Country and Western Room, with a doll made by Lila.

The Queen Anne Room.

SIERRA MESA LODGE, P.O. Box 463, Fort Stanton Road, Alto, NM 88312; (505) 336-4515; Larry and Lila Goodman, owners. Open all year. Five rooms, all with private baths. Rates: $75, single; $85, double, including full breakfast and afternoon tea. Children over 14 accepted; no pets; no smoking. Visa/MasterCard/Discover. Hot tub on premises. Skiing, golf (guest discounts), swimming, fishing, high-stakes horseracing, galleries, and hiking nearby.

DIRECTIONS: From Ruidoso, take Hwy. 48 past mile marker 9 and turn right on Ft. Stanton Rd. Inn is 2 miles down on the left.

Left, below. *Breakfast is served, silver and all.*

The East Room, used as a common room.

EATON HOUSE B&B INN

Bird watching paradise

The Eaton House, in Socorro, lies in the middle Rio Grande Valley of New Mexico. Surrounded by rich wildlife refuges such as the Bosque Del Apache and the Cibola National Forest, this area is one of the best bird watching spots in New Mexico.

Innkeeper Anna Appleby recalls one particular day when she drove the region and sighted eighty-seven species of birds in a twelve-hour span!

In addition to the helpful bird guides available at The Eaton House, guests can also observe, right in their back yard, such feathered visitors as cedar waxwings, Western tanagers, lazuli buntings, and countless varieties of exotic "hummers."

While the adobe exterior is distinctly Southwest, with a shady portal in back, most of the interior has a Victorian country flavor. Anna and her husband, Tom

Left.The Colonel Eaton Room.

Harper, have filled the dining room, sitting room, and four guest rooms with family heirlooms and furniture built by local artisans. The Daughter's Room features a claw footed tub and two beds built eighty years ago for twin daughters. In the Colonel Eaton Room is a high, four-poster bed hung with exquisite Westminster lace imported from England.

Early birders are packed off with a basket of coffee, juice, and homemade sweet rolls. They can also return for a hearty family style breakfast later in the morning. Using all organic ingredients, Anna's tasty specialties include Memorable Breakfast Soufflé, with brioche and peppered bacon on the side, or blue corn pancakes topped by piñon nuts and pomegranate syrup, along with turkey-chile sausages and a banana-fruit sundae.

THE EATON HOUSE BED & BREAKFAST INN, 403 Eaton Avenue, P.O. Box 536, Socorro, NM 87801; (505) 835-1067; Anna M. Appleby and Tom Harper, owners. Open all year. Four rooms, all with private baths. Rates: $75 to $85 in summer, including continental breakfast; $85 to $95 in winter, including full gourmet breakfast. Young adults 14 and over accepted; no pets; no smoking; wheelchair access to one room. Val Verde Steakhouse, Owl Bar and Cafe, El Sombrero, and Don Juan's recommended for dining.

DIRECTIONS: From I-25 south or north, take Exit 147. After traffic light at Hwy. 60, take first left turn on McCutcheon St. Drive 4 blocks to dead-end, then turn left on Eaton Ave. Inn is on right.

Southwestern ranch style.

THE GALISTEO INN

A 250-year-old hacienda

Nestled in a rural hamlet of low-walled adobes, The Galisteo Inn is a delightful haven. Owners Joanna Kaufman and Wayne Aarniokoski have managed to strike the perfect balance between rustic provinciality and luxurious sophistication.

This two hundred-fifty-year-old hacienda was once the estate of the region's original Spanish settlers. A Territorial adobe trimmed in Guadalupe blue, the inn boasts handsome viga-and-latilla ceilings, kiva fireplaces, plank and Mexican tile floors. Across a broad expanse of lawn in front, giant old cottonwoods sway with the wind.

Sprawled on eight acres of grounds is the main hacienda, plus numerous adobe cottages, a fifty-foot heated pool and hot tub, and, further down a gravel path, a duck pond and horse stables. A hammock swings over the tranquil pond, while ducks and geese waddle about.

In the hacienda, guests enter a striking *sala*, or entry hall that is the epitome of old New Mexico: rustic handcrafted furnishings, warm wood floors, saddle, and full Indian headdress are on display. Often a sleeping cat—either Ruby or Murphy—completes the idyllic picture.

Most of the guest rooms, named after local trees, are found in the main hacienda. They range in size from small singles to capacious suites, many with creamy feather quilts and plush towels. There is also a large living room full of books and plump sofas.

Left, above. *The Sala, or entry hall.* Below. *The Cottonwood Room.*

The gourmet Southwestern dinners at Galisteo Inn are not to be missed. A sample menu: brie quesadillas topped by mango, tomato and tomatillo salsa, followed by chicken soup with chiles, roasted tomato and lime; then, for the main course, perhaps chipotle shrimp with corn cakes, and an apple raspberry cobbler for dessert. And if you are still hungry the next morning, the homebaked croissants will be among the best you've ever encountered.

THE GALISTEO INN, HC 75 Box 4, Galisteo, NM 87540; (505) 982-1506; Wayne Aarniokoski and Joanna Kaufman, owners. Open February to December. Twelve rooms, including 9 doubles and 3 singles; 8 rooms with private bath, 4 with shared bath. Rates: $55 to $65, single; $90 to $165, double; extra person $15; includes continental plus breakfast and afternoon refreshments. Children over 12 welcome; no pets; smoking allowed outside only; Spanish spoken; some wheelchair access. Visa/MasterCard/ Discover. Dining room, swimming pool (open May to Oct.), hot tub, sauna, and mountain bikes on premises. Massage, horseback riding, and gourmet dinners available at extra charge.

DIRECTIONS: From Albuquerque, take I-40 east to Moriarty, then Hwy. 41 north to Galisteo. Inn is just northeast of the main intersection on an unmarked sidestreet to the right of Hwy. 41. From Santa Fe take I-25 north to Hwy 285 south to Hwy. 41 south to Galisteo.

The warm, inviting Common Room and Library.

CORRALES INN B&B

Unwind to classical music

Located a mere fifteen miles from Albuquerque, Corrales is a sleepy old town that dates back to the time of the pueblo Indians and Conquistadors. In the heart of the village is the Corrales Inn, a one-story adobe that was custom built in 1986 by Laura Warren and Mary Briault, both former schoolteachers.

They designed the inn around a central courtyard, with their private quarters in one wing, the breakfast room and living room in the second wing, and six clean, uncluttered bedrooms in the third wing. Three of the guest rooms feature Southwest décor, while the other three vary from Victorian to Oriental to Hot-Air Balloon themes. In the courtyard are willow chairs, a trickling fountain, and hot tub.

Classical music plays in the common room—a very comfortable place to unwind. Big, soft couches form a cozy horseshoe facing toward the kiva fireplace. Guests can help themselves to a glass of sherry and any number of games. An interesting collection of exotic masks (mostly from Mexico), antique iron keys, and original artwork cover the walls. And over two thousand books on every imaginable subject fill the floor-to-ceiling shelves.

Mary and Laura each have a calm, low-key nature that adds to the restfulness of the inn. They are well-traveled, educated hosts who are sensitive to their guests needs and give them a good deal of privacy. Shang, their gentle Sharp-pei dog, makes periodic rounds to greet everyone.

For eleven years, Mary and Laura ran the Monk's Refectory, a gourmet restaurant next door to the inn. Although they are no longer involved in the restaurant, their sublime breakfasts—blueberry pancakes, bacon, and bananas sautéed in the French manner, for example—reflect their expert culinary background.

The Corrales Inn is truly an oasis of civility.

CORRALES INN BED & BREAKFAST, 58 Perea Road, P.O. Box 1361, Corrales, NM 87048; (505) 897-4422; Mary Briault and Laura Warren, owners. Open all year. Six rooms, all with private baths; 1 room with fireplace. Rates: $55, single; $65 to $75, double, including full breakfast. Children accepted; pets accepted; smoking limited; French spoken; wheelchair access. Hot tub on premises. Rancho de Corrales, Casa Vieja, Monks Refectory and Desert Rose recommended for dining. Fine walks in the Bosque; birdwatching, horseback riding, crafts, arts, and clothing shops nearby.

DIRECTIONS: From I-40, take North Coors exit and drive 10 miles to Corrales stoplight. (Coors Rd. becomes Corrales Rd.) Continue 2.7 miles just past school and turn left on Perea Rd. Inn is behind Monks Refectory.

Room #5.

Room #2.

ALEXANDER'S INN

Utterly charming

It is impossible to avoid using the word "charming" to describe Alexander's Inn. It just slips out of your mouth when you walk through the door.

The red brick foundation and brown shingled roof of this 1903 country cottage is an uncommon sight in adobe-filled Santa Fe. Lilac trees frame the entry and envelop the house in a sweet springtime perfume. Inside, these and other colorful flowers are everywhere, contrasting nicely against the cottage white and periwinkle-trimmed walls.

Battenberg lace pillows, Dhurrie rugs, and light wood floors further enhance the fresh, inviting look of the interior. Sunlight streams through a plant-filled common room, where there are rustic wicker chairs, a wood stove, and freshly baked cookies or chips and salsa on the table. Out back is a wooden deck and lawn shaded by more lilacs, wisteria, and apricot trees.

Room Number Five, downstairs, is one favorite, with

Left, above. A leisurely breakfast on the deck is hard to forget. Below. Manager Jo Schneider, left, and owner Carolyn Lee, right.

its four-poster bed, fireplace, stained-glass window, loveseat, and clawfooted tub. Up a narrow flight of stairs are three cozy, romantic bedrooms that feature angled ceilings, dormer windows, and Laura Ashley touches. A separate adobe house behind the inn contains a newly added spacious suite.

Breakfast, taken out on the deck in nice weather, is an ample continental buffet of homemade breads or muffins, homemade granola, yogurt, fresh fruit, juice, and freshly ground coffee.

Owner Carolyn Lee (the inn is named after her son) and manager Mary Jo Schneider are young, easygoing innkeepers who encourage you to feel at home. It's the kind of place where you feel comfortable stepping into the kitchen to fix some late-night tea . . . or perhaps helping yourself to that one last cookie.

Alexander's Inn is only a few blocks from Santa Fe's downtown Plaza.

ALEXANDER'S INN, 529 East Palace Avenue, Santa Fe, NM 87501; (505) 986-1431; Carolyn Lee, owner; Mary Jo Schneider, manager. Open all year. Six rooms: 4 with private baths, 2 with shared bath; 2 rooms with fireplaces. Rates: $70 to $145; extra person $15; includes continental plus breakfast and afternoon refreshments. Complimentary bicycles and guest membership at health club provided. Children over 6 accepted; pets not usually accepted; no smoking; French spoken. Visa/MasterCard. Theatre, dance, skiing, river rafting, and golf nearby.

DIRECTIONS: From I-25, exit at Old Pecos Trail, which turns into Old Santa Fe Trail. Turn right on Paseo de Peralta, then right on Palace Ave. Inn is 2 blocks up on left.

Owners Louise Stewart and Pat Walter.

GRANT CORNER INN

Breakfast delights

After ordering her breakfast, the guest leaned toward her companion and said, excitedly, "I can hardly wait. . .I remember breakfast so clearly from the last time I was here."

Judging from the subsequent breakfast—apple corn-meal pancakes, bacon, fresh fruit frappés, and three kinds of muffins (chocolate chip, coconut lemon, and carrot)—these types of comments must be heard often at the Grant Corner Inn. Open to the public for weekend brunches, the inn received so many requests for recipes that they published a very successful cookbook.

Breakfast is one of many reasons why Grant Corner Inn is so well known in the Southwest. Situated only two blocks from Santa Fe's downtown plaza, it is conveniently located. Visitors frequently pass by the white picket fence and stop to look at the three-story 1905 colonial house, its gables veiled by delicate shade trees. A wrap-around porch and vine-covered gazebo at the entry add to its appeal.

The interior is mostly American Victorian, with an abundance of antiques, brass and four-poster beds, patchwork quilts, and ceiling fans in the bedrooms. Guests get acquainted over wine and cheese and crackers in the downstairs Wedgewood-blue parlor and dining room.

Grant Corner Inn is also a safe bet for people who want to try an old-fashioned bed and breakfast without

Left, below. *Room #7.*

losing the professional feel of a hotel. Owner Louise Stewart has a hotel business background (she grew up at the Camelback Inn in Scottsdale, built by her father) that is evident throughout the inn, from the smooth graciousness of her staff to the little amenities—personalized soaps, chocolates on the pillows, fruit baskets, welcome notes, TVs, and phones. She and her husband, Pat Walter (who is usually found in the kitchen whipping up breakfast) have been operating the inn since 1982.

GRANT CORNER INN, 122 Grant Avenue, Santa Fe, NM 87501; (505) 983-6678; Louise Stewart and Pat Walter, owners. Open all year. Thirteen rooms, including a separate 2-bedroom townhouse. Seven rooms with private baths; 6 rooms with 3 shared baths. Rates: $60 to $135, including full breakfast and afternoon wine and cheese. Children over 6 accepted; no pets; smoking on porch only; Spanish spoken. Visa/MasterCard. Museum of Fine Arts, Palace of the Governors, Santa Fe Plaza, shops, and galleries nearby.

DIRECTIONS: From I-25, exit at St. Francis St. and drive north for 3 miles. Turn right on Alameda and drive west 6 miles. Turn left on Guadalupe, then right on Johnson. Inn is 1 mile down on corner of Johnson and Grant.

Breakfast of apple-cornmeal pancakes is served on the porch.

EL PARADERO

A welcoming atmosphere

Built in the early 1800s and representing a mix of Spanish, Territorial, and Victorian eras, this former farmhouse in Santa Fe holds a great deal of architectural interest. Thom and Ouida MacGregor (Ouida is an architect and planner) performed a loving renovation on the structure. The walls, for instance, were restored with a mixture of buttermilk and sand, which gives the surface a nice grainy texture that changes color throughout the day.

But it's the welcoming atmosphere of El Paradero— meaning "stopping place"—that makes a stay here most memorable. A warm living room, breakfast room, and flowery patio provide ample gathering areas. Thom, Ouida, and their staff are friendly and unpretentious, greeting their guests with cider, tea, and snacks in the afternoon. And their abundance of resident pets—two dogs and a cat—are in droll attendance. Ouida says that Mr. Big, their cat, will gladly stay over with guests, and, she adds, with a twinkle in her eye, "He particularly likes to sleep with women."

Ten comfortable Southwest-style guest rooms, some with fireplaces, are in the main building. The most luxurious rooms are upstairs, featuring saltillo tiled floors and tiled baths. Two more Victorian-style suites are found down the block in a separate cottage.

A full breakfast is served in a skylit room amid hanging ferns. The menu includes such unique entrées as *calabasita* frittatas (made with squash, corn, cheese, green chiles, and cilantro) and maple nut muffins, or gingerbread pancakes with lemon sauce, or cinnamon croissant French toast.

Because many people come to Santa Fe nowadays for alternative healing reasons, Ouida says their inn tries to cater to environmentally sensitive products, wool and cotton fabrics, and feather pillows. "Nothing in our inn is artificial."

EL PARADERO, 220 West Manhattan, Santa Fe, NM 87501; (505) 988-1177; Ouida MacGregor and Thom Allen, owners. Open all year. Fourteen rooms, including 2 suites: 10 rooms with private baths, 4 with shared baths; some rooms with fireplaces. Rates: $40 to $130, single; $50 to $130, double, including full breakfast and afternoon refreshments. Children over 4 accepted; pets accepted by arrangement; no smoking; Spanish spoken. No credit cards. Summer opera and chamber music; year-round theatre and arts nearby.

DIRECTIONS: From I-25, take the Old Pecos Trail exit into Santa Fe. Turn left on Paseo de Peralta, then right on Galisteo. Take the first left at Manhattan.

Left, below. *Breakfast room.*

The Piño Suite.

Room No. 6 being visited by Echo, Mr. Bean, and Mr. Big, the inn's resident pets.

The lap pool.

DOS CASAS VIEJAS

Classic Santa Fe

Dos Casas Viejas, which means "two old houses," embodies classic Santa Fe—the old Southwest blended with touches of modern-day sophistication.

Inside the one-half-acre walled compound are two adobe buildings dating back to 1860. The first, with its original portal, viga ceilings, and Mexican tiled floors, houses a long common area that stretches from the lobby all the way outside to a forty-foot lap pool. The second adobe contains three differently-sized guest accommodations, each with its own private entrance, bricked patio, and kiva fireplace.

The interior is strikingly decorated with bold red accents everywhere. Against the rich flesh tones of the adobe walls in the common room are black and white cowhide chairs and vermilion sofas. Outside are red chile ristras and red geraniums. In one suite are luscious overtones of red; even red bathroom tiles. But for all the red, it is not overdone; rather, it enhances the luxurious feel of the inn.

Owner Jois (who is, not surprisingly, an interior decorator) and Irving Belfield had luxury in mind when they restored and opened Dos Casas Viejas in 1990. The guest quarters are furnished with real Southwest antiques and artwork, down comforters and pillows (and hard-ironed sheets, no less), TVs, and telephones. And, says Jois, "We went out for the softest, thickest towels we could find." Arriving guests enjoy a glass of welcome wine and bowls of chile-flavored pistachios.

DOS CASAS VIEJAS, 610 Agua Fria Street, Santa Fe, NM 87501; (505) 983-1636; Irving and Jois Belfield, owners. Open all year. Six rooms: 2 suites, 1 mini-suite and 2 rooms, all with private baths and fireplaces. Rates: $125 to $185, including welcome refreshments and deluxe continental breakfast. Lap pool on premises. Children not encouraged; no pets; no smoking. Visa/MasterCard. Escalera, Santacafe, Julian's, and Paul's recommended for dining. Folk Art Museum and galleries nearby.

DIRECTIONS: From I-25, exit at St. Francis Blvd. Drive 3.8 miles north to Agua Fria St. and turn right. Inn is 2 blocks up.

Left. *Room No. 3 is a mini suite.*

The bedroom of a suite.

The buildings are set in a courtyard.

CANYON ROAD CASITAS

On shoppers' row

Any serious shopper in Santa Fe is bound to wind up on Canyon Road, a narrow drive on the east side of town. Its seven-block length is lined with galleries, cafés, and little shops that could easily take a full day to explore.

One of the most intriguing shops along Canyon Road is Quilts Ltd., which specializes in American patchwork quilts, pillows, and other unusual textiles. And hidden behind the shop are two private adobe casitas.

The casitas share a peaceful brick courtyard enclosed by adobe walls and vining wisteria. The suite is the

Left. *The dining area of a suite.*

largest of the two, with a bedroom, kitchen, dining room, and smaller bedroom that has a fold-out futon. Its dining room is quite unique: the rustic brick floor, skylight-and-latilla roof, and shutters opening onto the courtyard give the room a sunny feel of the outdoors.

Both casitas have fireplaces and beautiful handmade quilts on the feather beds. The continental breakfast is self-serve: all the fixings, plus welcome wine and appetizers are found in a refrigerator.

The same women who run the quilt shop also manage the casitas. But with no resident innkeeper, these accommodations are for more independent guests who prefer the privacy of an unhosted bed and breakfast and the convenience of having Santa Fe's shops, cafés, and galleries right at their doorstep. The main plaza is only a short drive away.

CANYON ROAD CASITAS, 652 Canyon Road, Santa Fe, NM 87501; (800) 279-0755; Trisha Ambrose, owner. Open all year. Two casitas, both with kitchenettes and private baths. Rates: $85 to $169; including self-serve continental breakfast and welcome refreshments. Extra person $15. Children accepted; no pets; no smoking; Spanish spoken. Visa/MasterCard/American Express. Many shops, galleries and fine restaurants on Canyon Road.

DIRECTIONS: From I-25, exit at Old Pecos Trail and drive north into Santa Fe. Turn right on Paseo de Peralta, then right on Canyon Road. Inn is behind Quilts Ltd. shop on right.

LA POSADA DE CHIMAYÓ

Where time stood still

When Sue Farrington says her inn is out of the mainstream, she isn't kidding. Remotely situated on a dirt road in a little mountain town between Taos and Santa Fe, La Posada de Chimayó is about as removed from the twentieth century as you can get.

"The people who choose to stay in a place like this are usually adventuresome travelers and very interesting people," says Sue. Her two-suite adobe guesthouse and newly added two-bedroom adobe farmhouse are surrounded by the Sangre de Cristo foothills, where it is so quiet that the only sound you hear are crickets, high desert birds, and the occasional slap of a screen door.

The guesthouse is full of rural ambience, with a corrugated roof and inviting wooden swings over the earth-floored veranda. Inside, each suite has brick floors, a kiva fireplace in the living room, viga ceilings, leather chairs, and Mexican artwork. Guests can help themselves to afternoon wine in a small kitchen between the two suites. A sunset hike up the ridge behind the guesthouse affords arresting vistas of the whole Chimayó valley and its pink foothills.

One of the two suites.

The village of Chimayó is well-known for its long tradition of Spanish weavings.

For breakfast, Sue says, "We really stuff our guests." She serves scrumptious, hearty breakfasts of black beans, eggs and guacamole, or, in cold weather, bread pudding with ham.

LA POSADA DE CHIMAYÓ, P.O. Box 463, Chimayó, NM 87522; (505) 351-4605; Sue Farrington, owner. Open all year. Four rooms, all with private baths: 2 suites with fireplaces and 2 rooms in separate adobe farmhouse. Rates: $75 to $90, single; $85 to $110, double, including full breakfast and afternoon wine. Children over 12 welcome; pets permitted with prior approval; smoking outside only; Spanish spoken. Visa/MasterCard. Rancho de Chimayó and Anthony's at the Delta recommended for dining. Weavers, galleries, Santuario Church, cliff dwellings, and Indian pueblos nearby.

DIRECTIONS: Given upon confirmation.

Left. *A rustic 2-suite guest house.*   *Author/photographer Lucy Poshek relaxing on the porch.*

OLD TAOS GUESTHOUSE

Easygoing hosts put guests at ease

The Old Taos Guesthouse has a comfortable ambience that reflects the easygoing nature of its young owners, Tim and Leslie Reeves. As Tim will assure you, it's not the type of place where there are a lot of rules.

Their adobe hacienda sits on a rise overlooking Taos, two miles away. With over seven acres surrounding them, guests have plenty of strolling room. Horses graze peacefully in the alfalfa fields out back.

The Guesthouse began as a trapper's cabin one hundred-fifty years ago. Over the century, additional rooms were built around a courtyard. When Tim and Leslie moved to Taos from Santa Fe in 1989, they spent seven months renovating the structure.

The guest rooms, each with their own entrances around the grassy courtyard, are very Southwestern, with adobe walls, viga beamed ceilings and New Mexican furnishings. The Taos Suite and Sunset Suite are especially commodious. The Taos Suite features a raised platform bed, fireplace, and kitchen. Indian rugs are thrown over wood floors, and the Taos blue accents go well against the whitewashed walls. A sun-bleached cow skull—the quintessential Southwest symbol—hangs over the fireplace.

Skis and dried flowers hang in the homey breakfast room, where healthy continental breakfasts are served. Stewed applies, apricots, and cherries from their orchard are offered, along with strawberry bread, lemon nut muffins, and money bread.

Tim and Leslie are exceptionally friendly innkeepers who know how to put their guests at ease. As outdoor enthusiasts, they draw a lot of skiers during the winter. Says Leslie: "We love to hear ski stories and share the best wipe-outs." Their little girl Malia is equally engaging.

On Christmas Eve, over two hundred-fifty luminarios lead up to their hacienda, filling the night with a special glow.

Left, above. *The rustic Sunset Suite.* Below. *The Taos Suite.*

A stunning view of the buildings from a field out back.

The courtyard.

OLD TAOS GUESTHOUSE, Box 6552, Taos, NM 87571; (505) 758-5448; Tim and Leslie Reeves, owners. Open all year. Seven rooms and suites, all with private baths; some rooms with fireplaces; one with kitchenette. Rates: $50 to $85, single; $60 to $95, double; extra person $10; includes healthy continental breakfast. Children welcome; no pets; smoking allowed outside only; Spanish and German spoken. Visa/MasterCard. Downhill and cross-country skiing, horseback riding, hiking, mountain biking, white-water rafting nearby.

DIRECTIONS: From Taos Plaza, take Hwy. 64 (Kit Carson Rd.) east for 1.2 miles. Turn right on Witt Rd. Inn is 1/2 mile down on right side at 1028 Witt Road.

The Beutler Room.

LA POSADA DE TAOS

Serene symmetry

You can't get much closer to Taos Plaza—the center of Taos—than at La Posada de Taos. Only a two-and-a-half block walk away, this gracious adobe hacienda offers a handy location and congenial accommodations.

Beyond the adobe walls, one first enters a courtyard that contains the inn's biggest surprise—a Japanese garden. Some of the rooms, including a separate honeymoon cottage, are centered around this serenely symmetrical courtyard.

The Southwest architecture of the inn blends well with the East Coast furniture of innkeeper Sue Smoot. In the living room, for instance, is an adobe fireplace (with a lovely raised tile hearth) and viga beamed ceiling, but with oak floors and traditional trappings. Volumes of books and magazines fill the floor-to-ceiling shelves.

Most of the cheerful, whitewashed bedrooms have fresh country quilts (with electric blankets during the winter), and wood-burning stoves or fireplaces. The Beutler Room, in the main house, is most spacious, with a tiled bath and Jacuzzi tub. The cozy Honeymoon cottage—La Casa de la Luna de Miel—has a double loft bed and sky-light for stargazing.

Sue prefers to call La Posada de Taos a "bed and hearty breakfast." Served family style at a long table with French doors opening to an enclosed garden, her breakfasts are indeed hearty. Breakfast burritos are one of Sue's specialties, as are frittatas, bread pudding, and a dish that could only be invented in the Southwest—prickly pear cactus quiche.

LA POSADA DE TAOS, P.O. Box 1118, Taos, NM 87571; (505) 758-8164; Sue Smoot, owner. Open all year. Six rooms, including separate honeymoon cottage; all rooms with private baths and fireplaces or woodburning stoves. Rates: $60 to $85, single; $65 to $95, double, including full breakfast. Children accepted; pets accepted; smoking okay. No credit cards. Short walk to Taos Plaza, restaurants, shops and art galleries.

DIRECTIONS: From Taos Plaza, drive west on Don Fernando for 2 blocks. Turn left on Mazanares, then right on Juanita. Inn is at end of street at 309 Juanita Lane.

Left. *Adobe cottage on the courtyard.*   *The cheerfully lit breakfast room.*

Homemade European pastries are served with the afternoon tea.

The French Room.

CASA EUROPA

Stunningly restored

This splendid two-hundred-year-old adobe is the Southwest with a European flair. The afternoon tea, for instance—delicate fruit tarts, mocha buttercreams, Black Forest torte, éclairs, cream puffs, and chocolate mousse cake—is an exquisite array traditionally found in the Old World.

The pastry chef behind these mouthwatering delicacies is owner Rudi Zwicker, who was born in Germany and trained at the Grand Hotel in Nuremburg. He and his wife Marcia ran a successful Colorado restaurant for two decades before moving to Taos and opening Casa Europa.

Their stunningly restored inn is filled with large, elegant bedrooms and common rooms, a beautifully curved adobe staircase, and an art gallery showcasing regional artwork. The addition of fourteen skylights and many windows have made the adobe unusually light and airy.

Bedrooms are gracefully appointed with a blend of European and Southwest antiques. The French Room, for example, features hand-hewn wood floors, a kiva fireplace, and an 1860 French brass bed. The upstairs sitting room is particularly exotic, its Mexican couches covered in Turkish rug upholstery.

In the winter, afternoon "tea" turns to more heartwarming treats—après-ski wine and cheese fondue, or pasta salads, or canapés. And breakfast, served in the dining room, is no small affair, either: mushrooms and asparagus quiche, vegetarian eggs Benedict layered with avocado and tomato, or perhaps sour cream and orange crêpes with spiced cherry sauce. Sometimes Rudi and Marcia go into the woods and collect their own wild chantrelle mushrooms to use for breakfast dishes. Last year they gathered a whopping two hundred pounds of mushrooms!

Casa Europa is situated on the outskirts of Taos with spacious views from the balconies.

CASA EUROPA BED & BREAKFAST INN & GALLERY, 157 Upper Ranchitos Road, Taos, NM 87571; (505) 758-9798; Rudi and Marcia Zwicker, owners. Open all year. Five rooms, all with private baths: some rooms with fireplaces; one room with Jacuzzi and steam shower. Rates: $75 to $105, including full breakfast and afternoon tea (hors d'oeuvres served during ski season). Children over 5 accepted; no pets; no smoking; German spoken. Visa/MasterCard. Art gallery on premises. Rio Grande, Taos Ski Valley and Martinez Hacienda nearby.

DIRECTIONS: From Hwy. 68 north, just before reaching Taos Plaza, turn left on Ranchitos Rd. (Hwy. 240) and drive west for 1.3 miles. Turn right on Upper Ranchitos Rd. Inn is on left.

Left, above. *The adobe inn from the front.* Below. *Afternoon tea is served in the decorative upstairs sitting room.*

CHEEK'S STEWART HOUSE GALLERY AND INN

Hand-built by an eccentric

It's easy to understand why there have been some near-accidents outside the Stewart House. Skiers driving to Taos Ski Valley catch one fleeting glimpse of this outlandish structure and slam on their brakes to make a U-turn. It looks at first like a fanciful little Western village, complete with stuffed sheep grazing out by the creek. Only upon closer inspection does one discover it is a bed and breakfast.

The house was hand-built in the early 70s by an eccentric artist who reclaimed parts of history from all over the West: hand-hewn logs that are three centuries old; vigas and doors from a convent; gates made from old harps and wooden shutters; volcanic rocks for the chimney. It really must be seen to be believed.

The guest rooms are scattered among several low wooden buildings. They all have various Western

The whole building complex is very rustic, with many surprises.

Left, above. The Log Room is a rustic masterpiece. Below. The aptly named Bordello Suite.

Bathroom of the Bordello Suite.

themes, from the Log Room, with its log walls and wood stove, to the Bordello, a wildly frilly Victorian confection of red velvet and cream lace. Dark masculine colors, a saddle, and other cowboy touches dominate the Texan Room.

Besides owning an art gallery in Taos, innkeepers Don and Mildred also have art for sale in the inn's living room, where guests gather for afternoon wine and appetizers. Breakfast—offered early during ski season—is served here too.

Mildred is the first to admit that the rusticity of the Stewart House is not for everybody. Their guests are mostly adventurous people who have a good sense of humor. Informality is the key here. In the wintertime, for instance, it is not unusual for Mildred to find her guests outside having snowball fights.

"We say that you're only a guest once—after that, your're part of our family," says Mildred.

DON & MILDRED CHEEK'S STEWART HOUSE GALLERY AND INN, P.O. Box 2326, Taos, NM 87571; (505) 776-2913; Don and Mildred Cheek, owners. Open all year. Six rooms, all with private baths; some rooms with fireplaces. Rates: $75 to $120, including full breakfast; extra person $15. Children limited; no pets; no smoking. Visa/MasterCard. Art gallery and hot tub on premises. Taos Ski Valley and Millicent Rogers Museum nearby.

DIRECTIONS: From Taos on Hwy. 64, drive north 5 miles to the blinking light. Turn right on Taos Ski Valley Rd. (Hwy. 150). Inn is 1/2 mile north on left.

The Gallery Lilac Suite.

Judie serves a family-style breakfast in a sunny breakfast room while Elliot sits with the guests. Some of their specialties include eggs Denise (made with smoked salmon, cream cheese and green onions) with pierogis on the side, or egg chile frittatas, Mexican morning rice, and fresh pears.

Although the inn is only two minutes from Taos Plaza, it has a semi-rural feeling. Facing an open field, guests enjoy an unobstructed view of snow-capped Taos Mountain from the patio. Only Pozzi Franzetti's fanciful sculpture (called, by no coincidence "The God of Bed & Breakfasts") hovers in the foreground.

AMERICAN ARTISTS GALLERY HOUSE, 132 Frontier Road, P.O. Box 584, Taos, NM 87571; (800) 532-2041; (505) 758-4446; Elliot and Judie Framan, owners. Open all year. Six rooms, all with private baths and fireplaces. Rates: $65 to $95, including full breakfast and afternoon refreshments. Extra person $15 to $25. Infants and children over 5 accepted; no pets; no smoking. Visa/MasterCard. Lambert's, Brett House, and Apple Tree recommended for dining. Art gallery and hot tub on premises. Taos Pueblo, Taos Plaza, and museums nearby.

DIRECTIONS: Coming north into Taos on Hwy. 68, turn right on Frontier Rd., just before the Ramada Inn. Inn is on right.

AMERICAN ARTISTS GALLERY

A B&B for art lovers

The whimsical statues in the front are the first hints that this inn is more than just a bed and breakfast. It is, in fact, a combination art gallery and inn run by art lovers Elliot and Judie Framan.

In addition to the main gallery, which also serves as a living room for guests, each bedroom is essentially its own gallery. Paintings and sculpture by respected Taos names such as R.C. Gorman, John Suazo, Amado Peña, and Ed Morgan are for sale throughout the inn.

Six guest rooms, divided into four low buildings, range from large suites to a tiny, sweet cottage that is surprisingly popular with more amorous guests. Most rooms feature hand-painted tilework, Mexican saltillo floors, kiva fireplaces, and furnishings made by Taos craftsmen.

The rooms reflect Elliot and Judie's enthusiasm for the abundance of artistic talent in Taos. They will often take their guests on personal guided tours of Taos and the studios of local artists.

The Framans are also proud to be running an environmentally sound inn, with a recycling program, biodegradable cleaning products, and drought-resistant garden. "The whole inn is green," says Judie.

Left, above. The adobe exterior. Below. Owner Elliot Froman sits at the head of the table.

Metal sculpture entitled "The God of Bed and Breakfasts."

CASA DE MARTINEZ INN

A wonderful B&B hidden away in a remote valley

Clorinda Sanchez recalls sitting around her woodburning stove when she was a child and listening to stories about her family's house. Built by Clorinda's great-grandparents in the 1860s, the Martinez home began as a *jacal*, or adobe hut. Room after room was added as more children came along. By 1912—the year New Mexico became a state—the *jacal* had grown into a long, two-story L-shaped building with double adobe walls and countless rooms.

Casa de Martinez was left to five sons in 1915, and, as was the Spanish custom then, each son inherited a different room. Clorinda and her husband spent years buying each section, piece by piece, and now it stands much as it was, but as a bed and breakfast with modern conveniences added.

The multiple sets of stairs and common rooms indicate that several families once lived there. Downstairs is a living room with Indian décor. The upstairs sitting room has a Mexican theme, with piñatas and colorful serapes. Another sunny parlor was recently built for guests to have their pre-breakfast coffee.

Each bedroom, decorated in a mixture of antique and modern furnishings, is named for the direction it faces: The Los Brazos Room, for instance, has a picturesque view from its balcony of the Brazos cliffs and El Chorro Falls. The Martinez Suite, downstairs, is most spacious, with a handsome 1912 fireplace in the sitting room.

The tiny village of Los Brazos (meaning "where the rivers fork") is very rural, with nothing but the sound of bleeting sheep in the background. Most of the residents in this remote valley are descendants of the original Spanish homesteaders. At an elevation of over seven thousand feet, the valley is surrounded by snow-capped mountains all year round.

Left, below. *The Martinez Suite.*

Upstairs hallway, facing Los Brazos Room.

Details in the Los Brazos Room.

CASA DE MARTINEZ BED & BREAKFAST INN, P.O. Box 96, Los Ojos, NM 87551; (505) 588-7858; Medardo and Clorinda Sanchez, owners. Open February to October. Seven rooms: 3 with private baths; 4 sharing 2 baths. Rates: $45 to $60, single; $55 to $75, double, including full breakfast. Well-behaved children over 3 1/2 accepted; no pets; no smoking; Spanish spoken. No credit cards. Fishing, cross-country skiing, woolen shops, El Chorro waterfall, and Toltec narrow gauge train nearby.

DIRECTIONS: Inn is 65 miles north of Espanola and 13 miles south of Chama on US 84. In historic district of Los Brazos, turn right off US 84 just north of Los Brazos River.

THE ALAMO, SAN ANTONIO

Texas

Richard Barnett's porcelain collection.

SUNSET HEIGHTS INN

Biggest breakfast spread ever!

Prepare yourself for the biggest breakfast spread you've ever had. A typical menu: caviar and cream cheese on cucumbers, grapefruit, stuffed crab with melon, shrimp and avocado with kiwi, and a mini-veal Cordon Blue. (These are just the starters, mind you.) The main dish might be eggs Benedict or Machakas—mesquite-smoked beef, onions and avocado topped with sour cream. And if you can make it this far without having to be carried out on a stretcher, there's still a dessert of angel food cake with raspberry yogurt. Of his five to eight-course feasts, owner-chef Richard Barnett says, simply, "I believe in a decent breakfast."

Richard's breakfasts reflect the grand style of his inn. The three-story brick home is flanked by lush palm trees, a pool, and Jacuzzi. Guests enter through two sets of Tiffany doors to a foyer of polished oak floors and walls. The dining room is particularly impressive, with its Tiffany lamp, and all-beveled glass in the doors, windows and built-in hutches. A crystal chandelier and grandfather clock grace the parlor. Richard's lifelong collection of porcelain statuettes and art nouveau bronzes are everywhere.

The Bridal-Executive Suite, upstairs, contains a two-person Jacuzzi in the all-marble bathroom. Or guests can opt for an old-fashioned, seven-foot tub in the Oriental Room which has views of the Juarez Mountains from the one-way mirror windows.

Left, below. *The Bridal/Executive suite does double duty.*

The splendid breakfasts show that Richard is clearly no stranger to food—among other businesses, he owns an El Paso restaurant. And he will, with advance notice, whip up five to ten-course gourmet dinners (How about flaming filet of elk?) at his inn.

Built in 1905, the home is located in the historic Sunset Heights district of El Paso, near downtown.

SUNSET HEIGHTS BED & BREAKFAST INN, 717 West Yandell Avenue, El Paso, TX 79902; (800) 767-8513; (915) 544-1743; R. Barnett and R. Martinez, owners. Open all year. Six rooms, all with private baths; one room with fireplace and 2-person jacuzzi tub. Rates: $70 to $165; $10 more for double occupancy; includes 5-8 course gourmet breakfast. No small children accepted; no pets; no smoking; Spanish spoken. Visa/MasterCard/American Express. Swimming pool and hot tub on premises. Catered gourmet dinners provided at extra charge. Museums, racetracks, and Juárez, Mexico nearby.

DIRECTIONS: From I-10, exit at Porfirio Diaz. Turn right on Yandell Ave. Inn is on the corner of Yandell and Randolph.

Stuffed crab is one of seven breakfast courses.

Declared a Texas Historic Landmark in 1991.

GALBRAITH HOUSE B&B

A showcase of exotic woods

The Galbraith House, a 1912 Craftsman-style home, is situated in the Plemons-Eakle Historic District of Amarillo. The original owner, H.W. Galbraith, was an Irish lumber magnate who built the home to showcase his exotic wood products. The three-inch-thick sliding doors are of Philippine mahogany. The parquet floors of the solarium are inlaid with patterns of cherry, pine, walnut, and oak. The library and staircase are paneled in mahogany.

Mary Jane and David Johnson lived in the house for thirteen years before turning it into a bed and breakfast. Mary Jane is an internationally famous soprano who made her professional opera debut with Pavarotti. Since her work requires her to travel so much, she and David decided to open their home to guests. Innkeeper

Left, above. *The front of the Craftsman-style house.* Below. *The American Room.*

Connie Brown, who has her own home just down the street, welcomes the guests.

Although the Johnsons now maintain another home in Amarillo, their furnishings and personal touches still prevail throughout the Galbraith House. An upstairs gallery contains photographs chronicling Mary Jane's operatic career as well as her prized Emmy Award. Posters of her performances, from Santa Fe to Milan, line the walls.

Every room features country quilts and a different color scheme. One of the most attractive rooms, though not necessarily the largest, is Taylor's, which is decorated in delicate violet and cream floral patterns.

Early-bird coffee appears on the upstairs landing in the morning. Breakfast, served in a cheery dining room with blue and white checkered tablecloths, is suited to the tastes of the guests, ranging from continental to full. Connie, who likes to bake, often serves pastries such as almond puffs or chocolate chip coffee cake, along with fruit, and—a guest favorite—southern-style biscuits and gravy.

GALBRAITH HOUSE BED & BREAKFAST, 1710 South Polk, Amarillo, TX 79102; (806) 374-0237; David and Mary Jane Johnson, owners; Connie Brown, innkeeper. Open all year. Five rooms, all with private baths. Rates: $60 to $70, including full breakfast and afternoon refreshments. Children accepted; pets allowed in garage; no smoking. All credit cards. Cactus Grill, Gardski, and Rudy Tequila's recommended for dining. Cadillac Ranch, Cowboy Morning Breakfast, outdoor musical drama "Texas."

DIRECTIONS: From I-40, take Washington St. exit and go north. Turn right on 17th St., then right on S. Polk. Inn is third house on right.

Taylor's Room.

MICHAEL'S

Hurricane proof

This graceful red brick mansion was built in 1915 by Hans Guldmann, Danish vice-consul and director of the South Texas Cotton Oil Company. Having made his fortune in cottonseed products, Guldmann bought a fleet of yachts and turned his Galveston home into a showplace during the 1920s.

The façade is a mix of Prairie and Italianate styles, with wide archways revealing wrap-around verandas on both levels. Built during a devastating hurricane in Galveston, the house has extra sturdy, thick glass in the windows and front door. Expansive lawns and big palms surround the mansion.

Inside, all is open and airy, with a few graceful furnishings and an uninterrupted expanse of polished oak floors. The white walls, wide entries, profusion of windows, and spare décor is like a breath of fresh air compared to the darker Victorians that dominate Galveston.

The ground floor includes a large foyer, living room, enclosed porch, dining room, and den. In the foyer is a unique free-standing mahogany staircase that leads up to the guest rooms on the second floor.

Michael's is not only named after Mikey, the owner

Left. The impressive free-standing stairway in the foyer.

and innkeeper, but it radiates her fresh, relaxed personality. She and her husband Allen, an attorney, have collected some fine Western art and Remington-like bronzes that reflect their native Texas heritage.

For breakfast, Mikey often fixes whole wheat Belgian waffles and lays out a variety of toppings, such as whipped cream, berries, syrup, and nuts.

MICHAEL'S, 1715 35th Street, Galveston, TX 77550; (409) 763-3760; Mikey Isbell, owner. Open all year. Four rooms sharing one large bath; 2 rooms have sinks; extra half-bath downstairs. Rates: $85, including full breakfast. Children over 12 accepted; no pets; smoking allowed outside only. Visa/MasterCard. Eight blocks to seawall and beach; Elissa sailing ship, historic homes, and museums nearby.

DIRECTIONS: I-45 south becomes Broadway upon entering Galveston. Turn right on 35th St. and drive 8 blocks past Ave. O. Inn is first driveway on right after stoplight.

The Umbrella Room is decorated with parasols.

THE GILDED THISTLE

Teddy Bear heaven

Helen Hanemann knows the name of every stuffed bear in the Gilded Thistle, which is amazing considering how many there are. If asked, she will take you around her foyer and parlor, where her furry friends are gathered by the scores, and introduce them: George Schultz, Blanche, Mr. Fricks, Boris from Russia, Black Bear Junior, and Mr. Winkleman, to name just a few. "We have two bears named Victoria," says Helen, adding, "Of course, we have to separate them—they fight." She points to a docile-looking bear named Dennis who sits with a cookie in his hand: "He causes me no trouble."

Helen's character is very much a part of The Gilded Thistle, an 1893 Victorian in the historic district of Galveston. Her collection of teddy bears, seashells, plates, porcelaiin, hand-made garlands, and family photos overflow from every shelf and corner. Memorabilia abounds.

Left, above. *Teddy Bears in the entrance hall.* Below. *Teddy bears in the guest rooms.*

As for her accommodations, Helen says, "I like to pamper my guests." She greets them in the afternoon with cold drinks and a snack tray; in the morning with a hearty Texas breakfast. A typical menu might include half a cantaloupe, strawberry compôte, two meats (including "kabash," or Polish sausage), scrambled eggs, hot biscuits with pear preserves, strawberry bread and "chewies"—her secret recipe.

Although the master bedroom is largest, with a four-poster bed and fireplace, the Umbrella room is most unusual, having bold autumn colors, an elaborately-carved bed, and big paper umbrellas suspended from one corner.

The many full-length windows are a peculiar feature of the Gilded Thistle. Property taxes used to be based on how many doors each home had, so people built windows instead. In the Umbrella room, for instance, the windows lift up from the floor and from there you step out to the porch.

THE GILDED THISTLE, 1805 Broadway, Galveston Island, TX 77550; (800) 654-9380 (409) 763-0194; Helen L. Hanemann, owner. Open all year. Three rooms: 1 with private bath; 2 with shared bath. Rates: $135 to $145, including morning coffee and juice tray at your door, full breakfast, and evening wine and cheese tray. No pets; smoking on verandas. Visa/MasterCard. Historic homes (Ashton Villa and Bishop's Palace) within walking distance; Strand District, museums, shops, and beaches nearby.

DIRECTIONS: I-45 south becomes Broadway upon entering Galveston. Inn is on right just past 19th St.

Kathleen's Room.

PATRICIAN B&B INN

An immaculate B&B inn

The Patrician Bed & Breakfast Inn is near downtown Houston in a convenient area known as the Museum District. Close at hand are all the major museums, parks, gardens, and libraries of Houston.

The three-story Colonial Revival mansion was built in 1919 by a prominent Houston attorney. Pat Thomas restored the home and turned it into an immaculate four-room inn. In addition to innkeeping, Pat also runs a reservation service called the Bed & Breakfast Society of Texas, so she really knows what her guests are looking for.

Different color schemes run throughout the well-tended house: the foyer is light pink; the solarium is all-white; the dining room has cool tones; the Ivey Room features green ivy patterns, while the Margaret Rose room has dark rose-colored walls. Two of the most attractive rooms are the downstairs parlor and

Left, below. *Lottie Dee's Room.*

Kathleen's Room, both in hunter green and butter-creamy white.

The antiques are tastefully appointed. In the Lottie Dee Room, which has its own balcony, is a turn-of-the-century burled walnut bed and a vanity from Argentina. The Margaret Rose room has a handsome Eastlake bed. Yellow rubber ducks peek out from clawfooted tubs in two rooms.

Pat has recently added a deck and fourteen-foot gazebo, which makes a nice setting for outdoor weddings. The white tiled solarium has French doors that can open out to the deck.

Each morning brings a generous breakfast of fresh-squeezed orange juice, fresh fruit, pear compôte, sticky buns, and perhaps creamy French toast with orange sauce.

PATRICIAN BED & BREAKFAST INN, 1200 Southmore Avenue, Houston, TX 77004; (800) 553-5797; (713) 523-1114; Pat H. Thomas, owner. Open all year. Four rooms, including one 2-room suite; all rooms with private baths. Rates: $50 to $70, single; $65 to $85, double, including full breakfast. Children accepted; no pets; no smoking. Visa/MasterCard/American Express. Cafe Noche, Kathy's and Black Labrador recommended for dining. Museum of Fine Arts, Houston Zoo and Gardens, Hermann Park, and Rice University nearby.

DIRECTIONS: From US 59 south, take Fannin exit just past downtown Houston. Turn left at second light which is Southmore. Inn is on corner of Southmore Ave. and San Jacinto. Cross San Jacinto and turn right into driveway.

The back porch, looking to the gazebo.

A beautiful Victorian wedding dress on display.

DURHAM HOUSE B&B INN

Guests arrive dressed-to-kill!

The Durham House, in historic Houston Heights, is a model of circa-1900 Victorian romance. Hearts and lace are everywhere. Guest rooms—especially the Honeymoon Suite, in the carriage house, and the Rose room, in the main house—are elegantly feminine, with creamy spreads, frilly pillows, heart-shaped sachets, dried flower wreaths, antique dresses, and fine lace curtains. Honeymoon couples enjoy complimentary champagne, and placed near every bed is a decadent chocolate truffle. Bicycles built-for-two are also available.

The soft peach and white classic Victorian exterior, outdoor gazebo, topiary swans, and large screened-in porch set the perfect tone for weddings, which inn-keeper Marguerite Swanson caters quite regularly. Her living room/parlor and dining room are well-designed for receptions.

But Marguerite's real delight is orchestrating murder mystery dinner parties—events which have earned her the nickname "Ms. Mystery." Several times a month, a dozen or more dinner guests arrive at the Durham House in the costume of their pre-assigned character and time period. They spend four hours wining, dining, and solving one of Marguerite's cleverly-written mysteries. As she says, "People always think of a murder mystery as a weekend. But an evening is just

Left, Below. *The Rose Room.*

as possible." Sherman, the basset hound, looks like he's ready to solve any mystery. All he needs is a Sherlock Holmes hat to complete his role.

Marguerite is well-known throughout Texas not only for her mystery evenings, but for her gracious manner and attentive hospitality. She has a remarkable memory for her guest's names, as well as their likes and dislikes. During the week, her inn draws many business guests, whereas on the weekends she accommodates what she affectionately calls the "Love Boat" people.

DURHAM HOUSE BED & BREAKFAST INN, 921 Heights Boulevard, Houston, TX 77008; (800) 722-8788 (713) 868-4654; Marguerite Swanson, owner. Open all year. Five rooms and suites: 3 rooms in main house, 2 rooms and 1 suite in separate carriage house; 5 1/2 baths. Rates: $50 to $65, single; $60 to $85, double, including full breakfast and afternoon refreshments. Infants and children over 12 accepted; no pets; no smoking; some German spoken. Visa/MasterCard/American Express. Listed on National Register of Historic Places. Historic homes, museums, shopping, nightclubs, and downtown Houston nearby.

DIRECTIONS: From downtown Houston take I-10 west to Heights-Studemont exit. Continue west on feeder road to Heights Blvd. and turn right. Inn is 6 blocks north on the left.

Central Hall and parlor.

TERRELL CASTLE B&B

British décor

While Edwin Terrell served as the American ambassador to Belgium in the 1890s, he was enthralled by the romantic castles of Europe. When Terrell returned home to Texas he commissioned a British architect to design a "castle for his bride" and their six children.

When Katherine Poulis and her daughter, Nancy Haley, bought the Castle in 1986, it had been turned into apartments and was in a sorry state. They spent months restoring it to its former grandeur.

The downstairs common areas are elegantly appointed with Victorian antiques from Katherine and Nancy's previous homes. In the central hall is a unique "coffin niche" with a fireplace, while an impressive white staircase sweeps above it. The fine parquet floors are covered with Oriental carpets. The parlor, library, and dining room also emanate from the central hall.

The guest quarters, most with British décor, meander all over the upper floors, with multiple hallways and stairs. Several rooms are large enough to accommodate families. The Terrell Suite is a popular choice, featuring a large bay window, fireplace, and its own sun room.

Breakfast can be had in the dining room at absolutely any time of the morning. (No kidding—from 7:30 to noon!) Huge bowls of fruit are served, along with tasty muffins and biscuits, eggs, sausage, and bacon. Then it's time to head to downtown San Antonio for a River Walk or tour of the Alamo.

TERRELL CASTLE BED AND BREAKFAST, 950 East Grayson Street, San Antonio, TX 78208; (800) 356-1605; (512) 271-9145; Nancy Jane Haley and Katherine M. Poulis, owners. Open all year. Nine rooms and suites: 7 rooms with private baths, 2 sharing a bath; some rooms with fireplaces. Rates: $70 to $85, single; $85 to $100, double; extra person $15 (no charge for children 6 and under); includes full breakfast. Children accepted; pets accepted; smoking allowed; Spanish, French and German spoken. Visa/MasterCard/American Express/Discover. About 20 blocks to the Alamo and River Walk.

DIRECTIONS: From US 281 (also called I-37) south, exit at Josephine-Grayson Sts. and turn left on Grayson. Inn is 6 blocks down on right.

The Tower Suite.

The Persian Suite describes this guest room perfectly.

FALLING PINES B&B INN

And then there's the Persian Suite

Now, *this* is a mansion. Situated in San Antonio's historic Monte Verde District, Falling Pines encompasses an entire residential block. Built in 1911, the magnificent brick and limestone mansion is distinguished by Italianate archways, abundant balconies, and pine trees towering in front.

The nine-thousand-square-foot interior is even more palatial. Quarter-cut oak paneling, Oriental carpets, and luxurious furnishings on the ground floor exude the somber grandeur of a baronial manor. In the music room is an 1860 Steinway piano; in the living room are luxurious silk couches; in the dining room are high, carved chairs. There is also a library and tiled solarium where breakfast is served.

Owner Bob Daubert, an oil businessman, and his wife Grace have artfully embellished the three second-floor guest rooms. One room contains a seventeenth-

Left, above. *A very imposing building.* Below. *Looking from the central hall to the music Room.*

century English cherry-wood sleigh bed. Another carries a masculine theme, while the third is serenely appointed in shades of cream.

But the crowning glory of Falling Pines is the Persian Suite on the third floor. What was formerly the attic ballroom has been transformed into a contemporary version of "Arabian Nights." Hundreds of yards of beige artist's canvas have been gathered and draped from every wall and ceiling, creating the effect of an enormous tent. A cream-colored bed seems to float out from the center, as does the free-standing shower in the bathroom (which, by the way, is a most remarkable bathroom). The all-neutral tones of cream, beige and brown throughout the suite are most striking. From one of its two balconies are views of downtown San Antonio.

In every room there are flowers and a decanter of brandy with cut crystal glasses. The full breakfast includes Bob's homemade strudel.

FALLING PINES B&B INN, 300 West French Place, San Antonio, TX 78212; (800) 880-4580; (512) 733-1998; Grace and Bob Daubert, owners. Open all year. Four rooms, including one suite; all rooms with private baths. Rates: $67 to $97, including full breakfast. Children over 10 accepted; no pets; no smoking; Spanish spoken. Visa/MasterCard/American Express. La Fonda and Paisano's recommended for dining. Guest memberships at country club included. San Pedro Park, San Antonio Zoo, and tennis center nearby.

DIRECTIONS: From US 281 (also called I-37), exit at Mulberry St. and drive west. Turn left on Belknap and follow to W. French Pl. Inn is large mansion on Belknap and French Pl.

The Crystal River Inn

Bed & Breakfast Lodgings
In the Spirit of
the Hill Country

The Frio Room.

CRYSTAL RIVER INN

The famous Texas Hill Country

At the Crystal River Inn each room is dedicated to a different river in the Texas Hill Country: the Frio, Pedernales, Colorado, Medina, Blanco, Guadalupe, Sabinal, Llano, Corrial, and Concho. Although the inn itself is not on the water, it's only an eight-block walk to the Crystal River, where you can lie along the banks and swim or float on an inner tube.

The front of the inn is distinguished by impressive white Corinthian columns and a second-story porch. Inside, all is cheerful and inviting: a chandelier, wood floors, and etched-glass doors in the foyer, and a comfortable front parlor filled with cream and cinnamon-colored antiques, vintage magazines, and many books.

Down the hall is a big breakfast room with a piano, wet bar, and full windows looking out to an extensive back yard and shady pecan trees. Guests can eat breakfast here or out by the gurgling fountain in a walled courtyard. On weekends, they enjoy such dishes as stuffed French toast with apricot sauce, or Bananas Foster Crêpes topped with Crème fraîche and walnuts.

Most of the guest rooms have an English country garden look, except for a few that are distinctly more Southwest. The Frio Room, on the ground floor, is especially pleasing, appointed in light blues, with a pastel country quilt hanging above the bed opposite a cozy wicker-filled sitting area. Additional rooms are in cottages across the street and behind the inn.

Owners Mike and Cathy Dillon have energetically assembled a series of weekend packages at the inn, such as murder mysteries, river canoeing, and country picnics. Between these events and frequent Hill Country festivals, things are hopping nearly every weekend.

CRYSTAL RIVER INN, 326 West Hopkins, San Marcos, TX 78666; (512) 396-3739; Cathy and Mike Dillon, owners. Open all year. Twelve rooms, 10 with private baths: 5 rooms in main house, 3 rooms in Young House, and 4 suites in Rock Cottage. Rates: $55 to $65 weekdays; $65 to $100 weekends, including full breakfast and afternoon refreshments; extra person $7.50 to $10. Children, pets, and smoking discouraged. Some Spanish spoken. All credit cards. Intertubing, bicycling, swimming, and fishing nearby.
DIRECTIONS: From I-35, take exit £205 (Hopkins) and drive west to downtown San Marcos. Inn is 3 blocks past courthouse on right.

The Kiehne House.

The Henke Suite.

COUNTRY COTTAGE INN

Admiral Nimitz was born here

The Country Cottage Inn actually consists of two separate stone houses in the heart of downtown Fredricksburg. Not only are they each historic treasures in their own right, they are extremely romantic, too.

The Nimitz Birthplace, is, as the name implies, the birthplace of Fleet Admiral Chester W. Nimitz. The little room where his mother gave birth to Nimitz is now a guest room, with letters and mementos lining the walls. The rest of the 1866 house is essentially unchanged, with thick rock walls, large stone fireplaces, and roughhewn antiques, such as a blacksmith bellows coffee table, cheese press, and flint threshing board. The only obvious updates are the bathrooms, which have whirlpool tubs for two, and unobtrusive kitchenettes. Mountain Laurel, a spacious upstairs loft, is also rustically atmospheric, featuring an eight-foot copper tub.

Built in 1850, the Kiehne House was the first two-

Left, above. *The Nimitz Birthplace.* Below. *The Nimitz Suite.*

story limestone house in Fredricksburg. Inside the two-foot-thick whitewashed walls are several suites with high ceilings and exposed rafters. As at the Nimitz Birthplace, there are so many unusual antiques, it's hard to take them all in.

In both houses, the furnishings are rustic, but all the modern comforts are here. Bathrobes, wine glasses, Laura Ashley linens, lamb's fleece mattress covers, candles in the bathrooms—they all create a romantic flavor that will make you glad this is an unhosted inn. (Guests check in at a nearby antique shop run by manager Jeffrey Webb.) A sprig of mistletoe has even been placed over every bed.

The refrigerators are well-stocked with wine, smoked meat, fruit, and wonderful sweet rolls from the local German bakeries. Just outside the door are the quaint shops and restaurants of downtown Fredricksburg.

COUNTRY COTTAGE INN, 249 East Main Street, Fredericksburg, TX 78624; (512) 997-8549; Mike and Jean Sudderth, owners; Ms. Jeffrey Webb, manager. Open all year. Seven rooms and suites, all with private baths and kitchenettes: 4 rooms in Kiehne House; 3 rooms in Nimitz Birthplace; some rooms have large whirlpool tubs and fireplaces. Rates: $70 to $130, including self-serve continental breakfast and welcome refreshments. Children accepted; no pets; no smoking. Visa/MasterCard. German restaurants, bakeries, shops, and Admiral Nimitz Museum within walking distance.

DIRECTIONS: Both inns are on Main Street (Hwy. 290) in downtown Fredericksburg. Country Cottage Inn is at 405 E. Main St. and Nimitz Birthplace is at 247 E. Main St. Check in at 249 E. Main St. (antique shop).

DELFORGE PLACE

A nautical theme throughout

Since Betsy Delforge comes from a long line of sea captains, she has decorated each room of her bed and breakfast in a different time period and corresponding mariner's theme: The Map Room highlights the clipper ship era; the American Room carries a Civil War theme; and the Quebec Suite features the American Revolution.

The second level, or Upper Deck, is reminiscent of a ship's prow outside, complete with a ship's wheel, sea flags that spell "Delforge Place," deck chairs, and a weather vane. Inside, all is light blue, with an aquarium and skylight in the bedroom, as well as a porthole mirror in the bathroom.

The Victorian house and its seafaring touches are a delight for history buffs. Nineteenth-century costumes, paintings, atlases, trunks, quilts, and literature surround guests in a lively slice of the past. The décor changes frequently because Betsy's antiques are kept circulating through museums.

Left, above. *The colorful Quebec Suite.* Below. *The equally colorful Map Room.*

Built by a German pioneer in 1898, the Delforge Place exudes the same "willkommen" ambience that predominates in the German town of Fredericksburg. The living room is called the "wohnkuche," or gathering room. House breakfast specialties include homemade German sour cream twists and Belgian pastries, as well as soft molasses cookies placed in the bedrooms.

The house still has its original windows and doors of beveled, stained, and etched glass. The front porch is inviting, with wicker chairs looking out across a quiet residential neighborhood. A flowered patio is in back.

In addition to running the Delforge Place with her family, Betsy creates Special Day Baskets, custom-made with different local foods, linens, and containers. Her collection of glass plates, antique trays, and china dishes used for the baskets are displayed in the dining room.

DELFORGE PLACE, Represented by Gästehaus Schmidt, 231 West Main Street, Fredericksburg, TX 78624; (512) 997-5612; Betsy and George Delforge, owners; Robert Delforge, manager. Open all year. Four suites, all with private baths; one room with kitchenette. Rates: $70 to $75, including full breakfast and afternoon refreshments. Children over 8 accepted; no pets; smoking allowed outside only; French and Spanish spoken. Visa/MasterCard/Discover. Hilltop Cafe, Bavarian Inn, and The Gallery recommended for dining. Tennis, swimming, vineyards, and Arabian horse ranches nearby.

DIRECTIONS: Given upon confirmation.

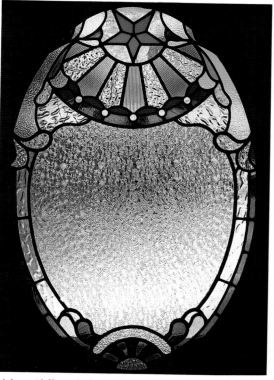

A beautifully etched and stained-glass window in the front door.

SOUTHARD HOUSE

An Austin landmark

An Austin landmark, the Southard House is an 1890 Greek Revival home that was originally only one story. In 1910 the whole building was raised, and an identical first level was built under it. A massive three-hundred-year-old oak tree stands guard before the two stately twin stories.

In the plant-filled front parlor the Southard family has thought up a clever alternative to the traditional guest register: a world map that has hundreds of pins and business cards indicating where all of their guest have come from.

The guest rooms are furnished with antiques—lots of iron and brass beds, as well as several clawfooted tubs with rubber ducks—and have intriguing names. The Treaty Oak Suite has an adjoining parlor that is quite spacious. Other rooms include Rolling Stone (an 1894 Austin weekly published by Will Porter), Lady Esther, Tickanwatic, and Moonlight. Down the street,

Left. *The dining room.*

a newly restored Victorian home, the Peppermint Inn, is favored for longer, unhosted stays.

The second-floor porch with its hanging plants and wicker chairs is a relaxing spot to while away the afternoon. One of the three pet cats—Andy, Beast, or Beauty—might join you. In the hallway, a butler's basket of extra toiletries has been thoughtfully placed out for forgetful guests.

The dining room boasts a long, handsome breakfast table, thought-provoking artwork, and an unusual wooden chandelier made from carved dragons that hold the lighbulbs in their mouths. The full breakfasts that are served here on the weekends often feature Mexican breakfasts called *migas*, made with corn tortillas, eggs, fresh tomatoes, and onions.

Located in a quiet neighborhood, Southard House is only nine blocks from the Colorado River walkways and Austin's renovated Sixth Street, full of shops and nightlife.

SOUTHARD HOUSE, 908 Blanco, Austin, TX 78703; (512) 474-4731; Jerry and Rejina Southard, owners. Open all year. Six rooms and suites, including suite with kitchenette in separate annex; all rooms with private baths. Rates: $59 to $159; $10 less for single occupancy; includes full breakfast on weekends, continental breakfast on weekends. Older children accepted; no pets; smoking allowed outside only. All credit cards. Colorado River (paddle boats and canoe rentals) and Sixth Street nightlife all within walking distance.

DIRECTIONS: From I-35, exit at 6th St. and drive west. After passing Congress and Lamar Sts. downtown, turn right on Blanco. Inn is on left.

THE McCALLUM HOUSE

An inn worth voting for

This 1907 Queen Anne house was built in Austin by A.N. and Jane Y. McCallum. A well-known suffragette, Jane lived here for nearly fifty years. When Roger and Nancy Danley bought it from the McCallum heirs in 1981, they were only its second owners. While restoring the building, they unearthed some of Jane's private papers from the attic floorboards, along with a big yellow banner that read: "8,000,000 WORKING WOMEN NEED THE VOTE."

Jane's old banner now hangs in the stair landing of the McCallum House, which has earned both a state historic marker (for Jane) and an Austin Landmark (for the house). Roger and Nancy have also named their lovely new loft suite after her.

Roger and Nancy, originally from the Midwest, are very congenial innkeepers who show genuine enthusiasm for their guests. Situated only six blocks from the University of Austin, they draw a lot of visiting faculty and researchers from all over the world.

Of breakfast, served family style in the dining room, Nancy says, "It's like a dinner party. We have great

Nancy and Roger Danley, owners.

Left, below. *Jane's Loft.*

Banner from Jane McCallum's suffragette days.

discussions on everything. It's amazing how much laughter there is." Indeed, their dining room looks almost like a salon, with dark wood paneling, a built-in window seat, and diamond-shaped windows. Along with a fruit bowl and egg dish, guests can indulge to their hearts content in fat-free, cholesterol-free muffins.

The Victorian-style guest rooms have their own kitchenettes, baths, sitting areas, TVs, phones, and breezy porches, plus a rather novel feature—an intercom system that runs from room to room. A private Garden Apartment, circa 1920s, is located in a second building right next door.

The surrounding neighborhood is pleasant, with plenty of little restaurants—including Tex-Mex food—and markets.

THE MCCALLUM HOUSE, 613 West 32nd Street, Austin, TX 78705; (512) 451-6744; Nancy and Roger Danley, owners. Open all year. Five rooms and suites, including separate Garden Apartment with kitchen; all rooms with private baths and kitchenettes. Rates: $55 to $85, single; $65 to $95, double, including full breakfast; extra person $15; Children over 7 welcome; no pets; smoking allowed outside only. Visa/MasterCard accepted only for holding room. Trudy's, Texas Star Cafe, and Monjuni's recommended for dining. LBJ Library, University of Texas, State Capitol, Zilker Park, theaters, and museums nearby.

DIRECTIONS: From I-35, take the 38-1/2 St. exit and drive west. Turn left (south) on Guadalupe St., then right (west) on 32nd St.

The McKie Room.

INN ON THE CREEK

Off the beaten track

The little town of Salado, in central Texas, was a thriving community in the 1890s—a favorite stopping place for the Indians, early traders, and stagecoaches. But because the ensuing railroad by-passed Salado, the town never grew much. Today, with a whopping fifteen hundred residents, the town remains much as it always was—green and unspoiled, with quaint shops and old homes along the shady banks of Salado Creek.

The Inn on the Creek is actually a collection of several historic buildings that were re-located from various parts of the county. The neatly-trimmed main house was built in 1892 and houses several stories of Victorian-style guest rooms and parlors. It is connected by a covered walkway to a second nineteenth-century structure where full country breakfasts and weekend suppers are served. Rockers and wicker chairs line the wrap-around verandas; in back they face the peaceful creek.

The guest rooms are named after people who made historic contributions to the community. Ceiling fans, turn-of-the-century photos, bedside chocolates, pretty soaps, and fat towels are found in each room. Some rooms have brass beds and claw-footed tubs. The McKie Room, on the top floor, is a guest favorite, with narrow angled ceilings leading to a charming reading

Left, above. *A complex of clapboard buildings.* Below. *The Fowler Room.*

alcove. Once you crawl inside and recline against the cozy window seat you may not want to leave that alcove.

Also on the twelve acres of grounds are two other guest cottages. Guests can stroll a quarter-mile up the creek or swim in its shallow, spring-fed waters.

The inn is a family operation run by Sue and Bob Whistler, and Suzi and Lynn Epps. With its relaxing country setting, variety of accommodations and a commodious dining room, weddings—about one a week—are a frequent occurrence.

INN ON THE CREEK, Center Circle, P.O. Box 858, Salado, TX 76571; (817) 947-5554; Suzi and Lynn Epps, Bob and Sue Whistler, owners. Open all year. Twelve rooms, all with private baths: 7 rooms in main house, 4 rooms in Reue House, and 1-bedroom cottage with kitchen. Rates: $70 to $100, including full breakfast. Children limited; no pets; no smoking; Spanish spoken. Visa/MasterCard. Dining room open for weekend dinners. Creek swimming, shopping, and gulf nearby.

DIRECTIONS: From I-35 south, take Salado-Holland exit. Continue on access road into downtown Salado. Turn east on Royal St., then left on Center Circle. Inn is 4 blocks down on left.

Classic rocking chairs on the porch.

The exquisite dining room.

RAPHAEL HOUSE

Artfully decorated

Owner Danna Cody.

On the National Historic Register, the Raphael House is one of the most enchantingly romantic and artfully decorated bed and breakfasts in Texas. The 1906 Neo-Classic Revival mansion was rescued from a severe state of decline by Danna Cody, a native of Ennis. Within less than a year she transformed the run-down home into a glistening treasure.

Classical music and the soft scent of potpourri drift through the rooms. Mahogany and heart pine inlays highlight the foyer. The dining room provides a sumptuous setting for Danna's lively murder mystery dinners. The living room is lushly draped with yards of luxurious damask curtains. What was formerly the smoking room is now an exotic library/den.

All of the bedrooms are equally wonderful. Fannie and Edmond's room features persimmon-colored walls and a floral canopied bed. Raymond's room has a crisp blue and white décor. Julia's Room shimmers with different shades of silky creams and ivories. Ernest's room is masculine, in hunter green, burgundy, and dark wood. And Wilhelmina's room looks like it's

Left. *The handsomely striking Fannie & Edmonds Room.*

straight out of a dreamy Ivory-Merchant film—layers of heavenly white lace pillows and white linens contrast against a dark oak headboard and armoire, while Battenburg lace curtains float from the windows.

Danna is a charming young woman with a ready smile and spirited sense of humor. Like the whole town of Ennis, she exudes a natural friendliness that makes the Raphael House so welcoming.

Since Ennis has a large Czech population, Danna often serves a "Tex-Czech" breakfast of fruit, home-made apple strudel, kolbase, eggs, and buttermilk biscuits.

RAPHAEL HOUSE, 500 West Ennis Avenue, Ennis, TX 75119; (214) 875-1555; Danna K. Cody, owner. Open all year. Six rooms, all with private baths. Rates: $52 to $80, single; $65 to $95, double, including full "Tex-Czech" breakfast. Children accepted at host's discretion; no pets; no smoking; Spanish spoken. All credit cards. Kirkpatrick's, City Grill, Francisco's, and Bubba's recommended for dining. Guest privileges at Colonial Tennis and Health Club. Many year-round festivals in area.

DIRECTIONS: From Dallas, follow I-45 south. Take exit £251 and drive west one mile on Ennis Ave. Inn is on corner of Preston St. and Ennis Ave.

The lobby.

The lawn slopes gently down to the Paluxy River.

INN ON THE RIVER

Just what the doctor ordered

When the Inn on the River first opened as Dr. Snyder's Drugless Health Sanitarium back in 1919, guests were prescribed a dose of mineral water baths, healthful meals, and lots of relaxation. Today the formula is pretty much the same, only now the Craftsman-style inn has modern amenities and twenty-two impeccable, individually decorated rooms. Black and white checkered floors and rattan furnishings lend a fresh English-colony look to the lobby. The halls of all three wings are hung with beautiful country quilts.

But as nice as the rooms are, it's the restful grounds that set this inn apart. Massive, gnarled three-hundred-year-old oak trees—perhaps the most beautiful oaks you will ever see—shade an expansive green lawn that slopes down to the Paluxy River. White Adirondack chairs are grouped invitingly here and there. A mineral water swimming pool and pavilion overlook the river. The innkeepers will even provide you with complimentary fishing poles.

Michael and Nancy Rosenthal, a very congenial couple with extensive backgrounds in the hotel industry, have recently taken over as innkeepers. They are enthusiastic about having guests in this lovely part of Texas. "Nancy and I have always wanted to work together and run an inn," says Michael.

Left, above. Riverside view of the inn. Below. Suite #1.

Nancy, a marvelous cook, whips up gourmet breakfasts which Michael serves to guests in the glassed-in dining room. A typical repast might include hot blackberry-peach cobbler, herbed scrambled eggs, potato-rosemary pancakes (a guest favorite), bacon, lemon bread, and puff pastry with almonds. The plates are often garnished with edible flowers which, Michael says, not many guests have the nerve to try.

Situated in a beautiful land of rolling green hills, the old-fashioned town square of Glen Rose can be reached from Dallas in an hour.

INN ON THE RIVER, 205 Barnard Street, P.O. Box 1417, Glen Rose, TX 76043; (817) 897-2101; Nancy and Michael Rosenthal, innkeepers. Open all year. Twenty-two rooms and suites, all with private baths. Rates: $90 to $135, including full breakfast and afternoon refreshments; $10 less for single. No children; no pets; no smoking; Spanish and French spoken. All credit cards. Mineral water swimming pool and conference center on premises. Bicycles and fishing poles provided. Fossil Rim Wildlife Park, Dinosaur Valley State Park, Texas Amphitheatre, Courthouse Square, and Scottish links golf course nearby.

DIRECTIONS: From Dallas-Ft. Worth, take Hwy. 67 or 144 to Glen Rose. Follow signs to central business district. Inn is 1/2 block from town square.

HOTEL ST. GERMAIN

Unsurpassed luxury

In a modern city like Dallas, better known for its concrete high-rises, the Hotel St. Germain is a rare jewel.

Built in 1906 just north of downtown Dallas, the three-story white house is actually a full service luxury hotel. It has only seven suites, but they are the most sumptuous accommodations you could possibly find. As for the rest of the interior, well . . . have you ever seen Versailles?

Elaborate chandeliers hang from the high ceilings of the entrance hall and dining room beyond. The tall windows are draped with rich fabrics copied from nineteenth-century French designs. The woodwork trim has been treated with a rich crackle-back effect, and all the floors are polished wood. Moss-green French antiques and Bordeaux red patterns blend exquisitely with gold accents. Some of the screens and tapestries are over two hundred years old. There is also a formal parlor, library, and an intimate New Orleans-style courtyard.

Left. *The monumental Suite Two.*

The St. Germain is the brainchild of Claire Heymann, a native of Louisiana, who recently saved the house from demolition and restored it to an unsurpassed state of luxury. The décor reflects her French-Creole background, and it is clear that no expense was spared.

In addition to a full-time concierge, valet parking, and turn-down service, the St. Germain also offers gourmet candlelight dinners served on seventy-five-year-old Limoges china by tuxedoed butlers. The butlers reappear in the morning to serve café au lait and homebaked pastries.

The second and third floors house seven suites, each one more lavish than the next. They all have canopied feather beds, elegant French antiques, working fireplaces, large pristine bathrooms (some with pedestal sinks and Jacuzzi tubs), Roger and Gallet soaps, and guest robes. Some of the balconies capture city views.

HOTEL ST. GERMAIN, 2516 Maple Avenue, Dallas, TX 75201; (214) 871-2516; Claire L. Heymann, owner. Open all year. AAA ◆◆◆◆ rating. Seven suites, all with private baths and fireplaces; some rooms with jacuzzi tubs. Rates: $200 to $600, including continental breakfast. Children not encouraged; no pets; smoking allowed; French and Spanish spoken. Visa/MasterCard/American Express. Dining room on premises open to the public on weekends; open to guests for dinner all week with advance notice. In heart of McKinney Avenue District, with 50 restaurants, 25 art galleries, and 25 antique shops within walking distance.

DIRECTIONS: Located just north of downtown Dallas between McKinney Ave. and Cedar Springs. Directions given upon confirmation.

The Mauve Room.

B&B TEXAS STYLE

A Prairie-style mansion

Of the few historic districts left in Dallas, there is a wide boulevard of Georgian, Prairie and Spanish mansions that was known as the "silk stocking" area in the early 1900s. Now on the National and State Historic Register, the avenue underwent a sharp decline in the 60s, and even though the surrounding neighborhood still has a struggle ahead, at least this grand block is enjoying a revival.

Kathy Davis has been opening her home to guests for the past ten years. Built in 1908 by C.H. Munger (the developer for the area), her Frank Lloyd Wright Prairie-style mansion is surrounded by stately live oaks and magnolia trees.

The front entry (note the leaded and beveled glass door) and the initial common areas—living room, music room, and dining room—have a formal air, with their high ceilings and elegant antiques. But the rest of the house, including the side entrance more often used by guests, is decidedly informal.

For all their elegance, the formal rooms look largely unused. As Kathy says, "Everyone always ends up in the kitchen."

She hosts a lot of convention people who are looking for a homier alternative to the typical high-rise hotels in Dallas. On weekdays, when her guest are usually in a hurry, she fixes a continental breakfast; on weekends they enjoy a full spread in the dining room.

On top of running her bed and breakfast and working another full time job, Kathy has also been active in the neighborhood's Historical Preservation Society. Having lived here for twenty years, she can point out the most glamorous mansions. Just down the street, for instance, is the Aldredge House, which was once the set for the popular series "Dallas."

REPRESENTED BY BED & BREAKFAST TEXAS STYLE, INC., 4224 West Red Bird Lane, Dallas, TX 75237; (214) 298-8586; Kathy Davis, owner. Open all year. Four rooms, all with private baths. Rates: $75, single; $85, double, including full breakfast on weekends; continental plus breakfast on weekdays. Children over 12 accepted; no pets; an occasional smoker okay. Visa/ MasterCard. Over 30 restaurants within 1/2 mile. Lake sailing, golfing, downtown Dallas nearby.

DIRECTIONS: Directions given upon confirmation.

RESERVATION SERVICES AND ASSOCIATIONS

ARIZONA

MI CASA SU CASA B&B ACCOMMODATIONS. Ruth Thomas
Young. P.O. Box 950, Tempe, AZ 85280; (602) 990-0682;
(800) 456-0682. Publishes a B&B guide with some pictures.

BED & BREAKFAST IN ARIZONA. P.O. Box 8628, Scottsdale,
AZ 85252; (602) 995-2831; (800) 266-7829.

BED & BREAKFAST SCOTTSDALE & THE WEST. George
Thompson. P.O. Box 3999, Prescott, AZ 86302; (602) 776-
1102.

ARIZONA ASSOCIATION OF BED & BREAKFAST INNS.
3661 N. Campbell Avenue, P.O. Box 237, Tucson, AZ 85719;
(602) 231-6777.

BISBEE B&B ASSOCIATION. Bob Watkins. 200 E. Vista,
Bisbee, AZ 85603; (800) 388-4388.

SEDONA B&B INNKEEPERS GUILD. Lynne Gillman. 80
Canyon Circle Drive, Sedona, AZ 86336; (602) 284-0082.

NEW MEXICO

BED & BREAKFASTS OF NEW MEXICO. P.O. Box 2805,
Santa Fe, NM 87504; (505) 982-3332.

THE TAOS BED & BREAKFAST ASSOCIATION. P.O. Box
2772, Taos, NM 87571; (505) 758-4747; (800) 876-7857.

TEXAS

GASTHAUS SCHMIDT RESERVATION SERVICE. Loretta
Schmidt. 231 W. Main Street, Fredericksburg, TX 78624;
(512) 997-5612.

BED & BREAKFAST OF FREDERICKSBURG. Kathy Kopp.
102 S. Cherry Street, TX 78624; (512) 997-4712.

BE MY GUEST. Helen Taylor. 402 W. Main, Fredericksburg,
TX 78624; (512) 997-7227.

BED & BREAKFAST SOCIETY OF TEXAS. Pat Thomas. 1200
Southmore Avenue, Houston, TX 77004; (713) 523-1114;
(800) 553-5797.

BED & BREAKFAST HOSTS OF SAN ANTONIO. Lavern and
Vicky Campbell. 166 Rockhill, San Antonio, TX 78209; (512)
824-8036; (800) 356-1605.

MI CASA SU CASA
**Bed & Breakfast
Directory 1991-93**
Arizona and the Southwest

BED & BREAKFAST TEXAS STYLE. Ruth Wilson. 4224 W.
Red Bird Lane, Dallas, TX 75237; (214) 298-8586.

BED & BREAKFAST OF WIMBERLEY TEXAS. Larry Latto-
mus. P.O. Box 589, Wimberley, TX 78676; (512) 847-9666.

SAND DOLLAR HOSPITALITY. Pat Hirsbrunner. 3605 Men-
denhall Dr., Corpus Christi, TX 78415; (512) 853-1222.

HISTORIC HOTEL ASSOCIATION OF TEXAS. 231 West Main,
Fredericksburg, TX 78624; (512) 997-3980.